Protocol Buffers Handbook

Getting deeper into Protobuf internals and its usage

Clément Jean

Protocol Buffers Handbook

Group Product Manager: Kunal Sawant

Publishing Product Manager: Akash Sharma

Book Project Manager: Manisha Singh

Senior Editor: Kinnari Chohan

Technical Editor: Vidhisha Patidar

Copy Editor: Safis Editing

Proofreader: Kinnari Chohan

Indexer: Rekha Nair

Production Designer: Prashant Ghare

DevRel Marketing Coordinator: Sonia Chauhan

First published: May 2024

Production reference: 1190424

Published by Packt Publishing Ltd.

Grosvenor House

11 St Paul's Square

Birmingham

B3 1RB, UK

ISBN 978-1-80512-467-2

www.packtpub.com

To my mother, Géraldine Seyte, and my father, Marc Jean, for their sacrifices and for exemplifying the power of determination and curiosity. To my wife, 李梦昕, for her unconditional love and support.

– Clément Jean

Contributors

About the author

Clément Jean is the CTO of Education for Ethiopia, a start-up focusing on educating K-12 students in Ethiopia. On top of that, he is also an online instructor (on Udemy, Linux Foundation, and others) teaching people about different kinds of technologies. In both his occupations, he deals with technologies such as Protobuf and gRPC and how to apply them to real-life use cases. His overall goal is to empower people through education and technology.

About the reviewer

Eugene Khabarov is a software engineer with more than 18 years of experience. For approximately half of his career, he worked with Microsoft SQL Server, and he spent the other half with Golang, building gRPC and REST APIs, parsers, and generators. Several years ago, he started automating build processes with Bazel. He is passionate about software architecture, code performance, and team productivity.

Table of Contents

3

Describing Data with Protobuf Text Format   35

4

The Protobuf Compiler   47

5

Serialization Internals   71

6

Schema Evolution over Time   93

7

Implementing the Address Book in Go   107

Preface

In today's distributed world, a lot of us are interacting with APIs. Usually, these APIs are REST APIs, which accept and return JSON. There are, however, alternatives to the bulky and hard-to-process JSON data format. The main alternative is Protobuf. This book's goal is to teach you this more efficient data format in both theory and practice. From learning how to write proto files to learning how to write your own protoc plugin, passing by learning the internals of Protobuf serialization/deserialization, you will learn everything you need to know to become a Protobuf expert.

Who this book is for

This book is for both beginners and those who think that they already know how to use Protobuf. One of the main problems with Protobuf is that it looks simple on the surface, but becoming an expert takes a lot of time. Fortunately, I have condensed all my knowledge into this book, so you do not have to dig it up all by yourself. So, if you are interested in the internals of serialization/deserialization, how to use Protobuf for both small and large projects, and how to build tools around it, this book is for you.

What this book covers

Chapter 1, Serialization Primer, covers serialization and deserialization.

Chapter 2, Protobuf Is a Language, discusses Protobuf syntax.

Chapter 3, Describing Data with Protobuf Text Format, explains how and why to use Protobuf Text format.

Chapter 4, The Protobuf Compiler, discusses generating code and serializing/deserializing data with the compiler.

Chapter 5, Serialization Internals, explains every single part of the serialization/deserialization done by Protobuf.

Chapter 6, Schema Evolution over Time, covers how to evolve your Protobuf schema safely.

Chapter 7, Implementing an Address Book in Go, explains how to interact with generated code in Golang and build an address book.

Chapter 8, Implementing an Address Book in Python, explains how to interact with generated code in Python and build an address book.

Chapter 9, Developing a protoc Plugin in Go, shows you how to write a protoc plugin from scratch in Go.

Chapter 10, Advanced Build, covers the different ways to build your Protobuf projects.

To get the most out of this book

This book is in no way a Go or Python tutorial. You should be familiar with these languages before getting started. This will lower the mental load of having to learn both Protobuf and another programming language. I recommend you learn a bit of Go (see `https://go.dev/learn/`) since most of the code is in this language.

Software/hardware covered in the book	Operating system requirements
Python >= 3.10	Windows, macOS, or Linux
Go >= 1.21	
Protoc >= 25.0	

If you are using the digital version of this book, we advise you to type the code yourself or access the code from the book's GitHub repository (a link is available in the next section). Doing so will help you avoid any potential errors related to the copying and pasting of code.

Download the example code files

You can download the example code files for this book from GitHub at `https://github.com/PacktPublishing/Protocol-Buffers-Handbook`. If there's an update to the code, it will be updated in the GitHub repository.

We also have other code bundles from our rich catalog of books and videos available at `https://github.com/PacktPublishing/`. Check them out!

Conventions used

There are a number of text conventions used throughout this book.

`Code in text`: Indicates code words in text, database table names, folder names, filenames, file extensions, pathnames, dummy URLs, user input, and Twitter handles. Here is an example: "This should create a `buf.yaml` file in the `proto` directory."

A block of code is set as follows:

```
syntax = "proto3";
message Encoding {
   int32 i32 = 1;
}
```

When we wish to draw your attention to a particular part of a code block, the relevant lines or items are set in bold:

```
type Person_PhoneNumber_Type int32
const (
  Person_PhoneNumber_TYPE_UNSPECIFIED  Person_PhoneNumber_Type = 0
  Person_PhoneNumber_TYPE_MOBILE  Person_PhoneNumber_Type = 1
  Person_PhoneNumber_TYPE_HOME  Person_PhoneNumber_Type = 2
  Person_PhoneNumber_TYPE_WORK  Person_PhoneNumber_Type = 3
)
```

Any command-line input or output is written as follows:

```
$ cat int32.txtpb | protoc --encode=Encoding encoding.proto | hexdump
-C
```

Bold: Indicates a new term, an important word, or words that you see onscreen. For instance, words in menus or dialog boxes appear in **bold**. Here is an example: "The structure of the data is called the **data format**."

> Tips or important notes
> Appear like this.

Get in touch

Feedback from our readers is always welcome.

General feedback: If you have questions about any aspect of this book, email us at customercare@ packtpub.com and mention the book title in the subject of your message.

Errata: Although we have taken every care to ensure the accuracy of our content, mistakes do happen. If you have found a mistake in this book, we would be grateful if you would report this to us. Please visit www.packtpub.com/support/errata and fill in the form.

Piracy: If you come across any illegal copies of our works in any form on the internet, we would be grateful if you would provide us with the location address or website name. Please contact us at copyright@packtpub.com with a link to the material.

If you are interested in becoming an author: If there is a topic that you have expertise in and you are interested in either writing or contributing to a book, please visit authors.packtpub.com.

Share Your Thoughts

Once you've read *Protocol Buffers Handbook*, we'd love to hear your thoughts! Scan the QR code below to go straight to the Amazon review page for this book and share your feedback.

https://packt.link/r/1805124676

Your review is important to us and the tech community and will help us make sure we're delivering excellent quality content.

Download a free PDF copy of this book

Thanks for purchasing this book!

Do you like to read on the go but are unable to carry your print books everywhere?

Is your eBook purchase not compatible with the device of your choice?

Don't worry, now with every Packt book you get a DRM-free PDF version of that book at no cost.

Read anywhere, any place, on any device. Search, copy, and paste code from your favorite technical books directly into your application.

The perks don't stop there, you can get exclusive access to discounts, newsletters, and great free content in your inbox daily

Follow these simple steps to get the benefits:

1. Scan the QR code or visit the link below

https://packt.link/free-ebook/978-1-80512-467-2

2. Submit your proof of purchase
3. That's it! We'll send your free PDF and other benefits to your email directly

1
Serialization Primer

Welcome to the first chapter of this book: *Serialization Primer*. Whether you are experienced in serialization and deserialization or new to the concept, we are here to learn what these concepts are and how they relate to **Protocol Buffers** (**Protobuf**). So, let's get started!

At its heart, Protobuf is all about serialization and deserialization. So, before starting to write our own proto files, generate code, and use it in code, we will need to understand what Protobuf is used for and why it is used. In this primer, we will lay the foundations so that we can build up our knowledge of Protobuf on top of them.

In this chapter, we are going to cover the following topics:

- Serialization's goals
- Why use Protobuf?

At the end of this chapter, you will be confident about your knowledge of serialization and deserialization. You will understand what Protobuf is doing and why it is important to have such a data format in our software engineer toolbox.

Technical requirements

All the code examples that you will see in this section can be found under the directory called `chapter1` in the GitHub repository (`https://github.com/PacktPublishing/Protocol-Buffers-Handbook`).

Serialization's goals

Serialization and its counterpart, deserialization, enable us to handle data seamlessly across time and machines. This is highly relevant to current workloads because we have more and more data that we process in batches and we have more and more distributed systems that need to send data on the wire. In this section, we will dive a little bit deeper into serialization to understand how it can achieve encoding of data for later use.

How does it all work?

In order to process data across time and machines, we need to take data that is in **volatile memory** (memory that needs constant power in order to retain data) and save it to **non-volatile memory** (memory that retains stored information even after power is removed) or send data that is in volatile memory over the wire. And because we need to be able to make sense of the data that was saved to a file or sent over the wire, this data needs to have a certain structure.

The structure of the data is called the **data format**. It is a way of encoding data that is understood by the deserialization process in order to recreate the original data. Protobuf is one such data format.

Once this data is encoded in a certain way, we can save it to a file, send it across the network, and so on. And when the time comes to read this data, deserialization kicks in. It will take the data encoded following the data format rules (serialized data) and turn it back into data in volatile memory. *Figure 1.1* summarizes graphically the data lifecycle during serialization and deserialization.

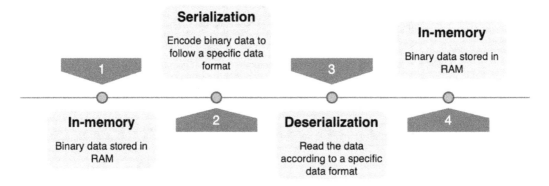

Figure 1.1 – Data lifecycle during serialization/deserialization

To summarize, in order to treat data across time and machines, we need to serialize it. This means that we need to take some sort of data and encode it with rules given by a specific data format. And after that, when we want to finally reuse the data, we deserialize the encoded data. This is the big picture of serialization and deserialization. Let us now see what the different data formats are and the metrics we can use in order to compare them.

The different data formats

As mentioned earlier in this chapter, a data format is a way of encoding data that can be interpreted by both the application engaged in serialization and the one involved in deserialization. There are multiple such formats, so it is impractical to list them all. However, we can distribute all of them into two categories:

- Text
- Binary

The most commonly used text data formats are JSON and XML. And for binary, there is Protobuf, but you might also know Apache Avro, Cap'n Proto, and others.

As with everything in software engineering, there are trade-offs for using one or the other. But before diving into these trade-offs, we need to understand the criteria on which we will base our comparison. Here are the criteria:

- **Serialized data size**: This is the size in bytes of the data after serialization
- **Availability of data**: This is the time it takes to deserialize data and use it in our code
- **Readability of data**: As humans, is it possible to read the serialized data without too much effort?

On top of that, certain data formats, such as Protobuf, rely on data schema to define the structure of the data. This brings another set of criteria that can be used to determine which data format is the best for your use case:

- **Type safety**: Can we make sure, at compile time, that the provided data is correct?
- **Readability of schema**: As humans, is it possible to read the schema without too much effort?

Let us now dive deeper into each criterion so that, later on, we can evaluate how Protobuf is doing against the competition.

Serialized data size

As the goal of serializing data is to send it across the wire or save it in non-volatile storage, there is a direct benefit of having a smaller payload size: we save disk space and/or bandwidth. In other words, this means that with the same amount of storage or bandwidth, the smaller payloads allow us to save/send more data.

Now, it is important to mention that, depending on the context, it is not always a good thing to have the smallest serialized data size. We are going to talk about this in the next subsection, but serializing to a smaller number of bytes means going away from the domain of human readability and going more toward the domain of machine readability.

An example of this can be illustrated if we take the following **JavaScript Object Notation (JSON)**:

```
{
  "person": {
    "name": "Clement"
  }
}
```

Let's compare it with the hexadecimal representation of Protobuf serialized data, which is the same as the previous data:

```
0a 07 43 6c 65 6d 65 6e 74
```

In the former code block, we can see the structure of the object clearly, but the latter is serialized as a smaller number of bytes (9 instead of 39 bytes). There is a trade-off here and while our example is not showing real-life data, we can get the idea of size saving bandwidth/storage while at the same time affecting readability.

Finally, serializing to a smaller number of bytes has another benefit which is that, since there are fewer bytes, we can go over all the data in less time and thus deserialize it faster. This is linked to the concept of availability of data, and this is what we are going to see now.

Availability of data

It is not a surprise that the bigger the number of bytes we deal with, the more processing power it will take. It is important to understand that deserialization is not free and that the more human-readable data is, the more data massaging will be required and thus more processing power will be used.

The availability of data is the time it takes between deserializing data and being able to act on it in code. If we were to write pseudo code for calculating the availability of data, we would have something like the following code block:

```
start = timeNowMs()
deserialize(data)
end = timeNowMs()
availability = end - start
```

It is as simple as this. Now, I believe we can agree that there is not much of a trade-off here. As impatient and/or performance-driven programmers, we prefer to lower the time it takes to deserialize data. The faster we get our data, the less it costs in bandwidth, developer time, and so on.

Readability of data

We mentioned the readability of data when we were talking about data serialization size. Let us now dive deeper into what it means. The readability of data refers to how easy it is to understand the structure of the data after serialization. While readability and understandability are subjective, there are formats that are inherently harder than others.

Text formats are generally easier to understand because they are designed for humans. In these formats, we want to be able to quickly edit values with a simple text editor. This is the case for XML, JSON, YAML, and others. Furthermore, the ownership of objects is clearly defined by nesting objects into other ones. All of this is very intuitive, and it makes the data human readable.

On the other hand, binary formats are designed to be read by computers. While it is feasible to read them with knowledge of the format and with some extra effort, the overall goal is to make the computer serialize/deserialize the data faster. Open such serialized data with a text editor and you will see, sometimes, it is not even possible to distinguish bytes. Instead, you would have to use tools such as hexdump to see the hexadecimal representation of the binary.

To summarize, the readability of data is a trade-off that mainly focuses on who the reader of the data is. If it is humans, go with text formats, and if it is machines, choose binary since they will be able to understand the data faster.

Type safety

As mentioned, some data formats rely on us to describe the data through schemas. If you have worked with JSON Schema or any other kind of schema, you know that we can explicitly set types to fields in order to limit the possible value. For example, say we have the following Protobuf schema (note that this is not correct because it is simplified):

```
message Person {
  string name;
}
```

With this Protobuf schema, we would be only able to set strings to the name field, not integers, floats, or others. On the other hand, say we add the following JSON (without JSON Schema):

```
{
  "person": {
    "name": "Clément"
  }
}
```

Nothing could stop us from setting names to a number, an array, or anything else.

This is the idea of type safety. Generally, we are trying to make the feedback loop for developers shorter. If we are setting the wrong type of data to a field, the earlier we know about it, the better. We should not be surprised by an exception when the code is in production.

However, it is important to note that there are also benefits to having dynamic typing. The main one is considered to be productivity. It is way faster to hack and iterate with JSON than to first define the schema, generate code, and import the generated code into the user code.

Once again, this is a trade-off. But this time, this is more about the maintainability and scale of your project. If you have a small project, why incur the overhead of having the extra complexity? But if you have a medium/large size project, you want to have a more rigorous process that will shorten the feedback loop for your developers.

Readability of schema

Finally, we can talk about the readability of the schema. Once again this is a subjective matter but there are points that are worth mentioning. The readability of the schema can be described as how easy it is to understand the relationship between objects and what the data represents.

Although it may appear that this applies solely to formats reliant on schemas, that's not the case. In reality, certain data formats are both the schema and the data they represent; JSON is an example of that. With nesting and typing of data, JSON can represent objects and their relationships, as well as what the internal data looks like. An example of that is the following JSON:

```
{
  "person": {
    "name": "Clément",
    "age": 100,
    "friends": [
      { "name": "Mark" },
      { "name": "John" }
    ]
  }
}
```

It describes a person whose name (a string) is `Clement`, whose `age` (a number) is `100`, and who has `friends` (an array) called `Mark` and `John`. As you can see, this is very intuitive. However, such a schema is not type-safe.

If we care about type safety, then we cannot choose to use straight JSON. We could set the wrong kind of data to the `name`, `age`, and `friends` fields. Furthermore, nothing indicates whether the objects in the `friends` fields are persons. This is mostly because, in JSON, we cannot create definitions of objects and use the types. All types are implicit.

Now, consider the following Protobuf schema (note that this is simplified):

```
message Person {
  string name;
  uint32 age;
  repeated Person friends; // equivalent of a list
}
```

Here we only have the schema, no data. However, we can quickly see that we have the explicit `string`, `uint32`, and `Person` types. This will prevent a lot of bugs by catching them at compile time. We simply cannot set a string to `age`, a number to `name`, and so on.

There are a lot more criteria for the readability of schema (boilerplate, language concepts, etc.) but we can probably agree on the fact that, for onboarding developers and maintaining the project, the type explicitness is important and will catch bugs early in the development process.

To summarize, we got ourselves another trade-off. The added complexity of an external schema might be too much for small projects. However, for medium and large projects the benefits that come with type-safe schema are worth the trouble of spending a little bit more time on schema definition.

You probably noticed, but there are a lot of trade-offs. All of these are fueled by business requirements but also by subjectivity. In this section, we saw the five important trade-offs that you need to consider before choosing a data format for your project. We saw that the size of serialized data is important to consider in order to save resources (e.g. storage and bandwidth). Then, we saw what is the availability of data in the context of deserialization and how the size of the serialized data will impact it. After that, we talked about the readability of serialized data. We said that whether the size of serialized data matters depends on who is reading the data. And finally, we talked about the readability and type safety of the schema. By having explicit types, we can make sure that only the right data gets serialized and deserialized, but it also makes reading the schema itself more approachable for new developers.

What about Protobuf?

So far, we have talked only a little bit about Protobuf. In this section, we are going to start explaining the advantages and disadvantages of Protobuf, and we are going to base the analysis on the criteria we saw in the previous section.

Serialized data size

Due to a lot of optimization and its binary format, Protobuf is one of the best formats in the area. This is especially true for serializing numbers. Let us see why this is the case.

The main reason why Protobuf is good at serializing data in a small number of bytes is that it is a binary format. In Protobuf, additional structural elements such as curly braces, colons, and brackets, typically found in formats such as JSON, XML, and YAML, are absent. Instead, Protobuf data is represented simply as raw bytes.

On top of that, we have optimization such as bitpacking and the use of varints, which help a lot. It makes serializing the same data to a smaller number of bytes easier than it would be if we naively serialized the binary representation of the data as it is in memory.

Bitpacking is a method that compresses data into as few bits as possible. Notice that we are talking about bits and not bytes here. You can think of bitpacking as trying to put multiple pieces of data in the same number of bytes. Here is an example of bitpacking in Protobuf:

```
0a   -> 0101 00000
     -> 010 is 2 (length-delimited type like string)
     -> 1 is the field tag
```

Do not worry too much about what this data is representing just yet. We are going to see that in *Chapter 5, Serialization*, when we talk about the internals of serialization. The most important thing to understand is that we have one byte containing two pieces of metadata. At scale, this reduces the payload size quite a lot.

Most of the integers in Protobuf are **varints**. Varints is short for **variable-size integers** and they map integers to different numbers of bytes. How this works is that the smaller values will get mapped to a smaller number of bytes and the bigger ones will get translated to a larger number of bytes. Let us see an example (`decimal -> byte(s) in hexadecimal`):

```
1 -> 01
128 -> 80 01
16,384 -> 80 80 01
...
```

As you can see, compared to fixed-size integers (four or eight bytes), it saves space in a lot of cases. However, this also can result in non-efficient compression of the data. We can also store a 32-bit number (normally 4 bytes) in 5 bytes. Here is an example of such a case:

```
2,147,483,647 (max 32-bit number value) -> ff ff ff ff 07
```

We have five bytes instead of four if we serialize with a fixed-size integer.

While we did not get into too much detail about the internals of serialization that make the serialized data size smaller, we learned about the two main optimizations that are used in Protobuf. We saw that it uses bitpacking to compress data into smaller amounts of bits. This is what Protobuf does to limit the impact of metadata on serialized data size. Then, we saw that Protobuf also uses varints. They map smaller integers to smaller numbers of bytes. This is how most integers are serialized in Protobuf.

Availability of data

Deserializing data in Protobuf is fast because we are parsing binary instead of text. Now, this is hard to demonstrate because it is highly dependent on the programming language you are using and the data you have. However, a study conducted by Auth0 (`https://auth0.com/blog/beating-json-performance-with-protobuf/`) showed that Protobuf, in their use case, has better availability than JSON.

What is interesting in this study is that they found that Protobuf messages were available in their JavaScript code in 4% less time than JSON. Now, this might seem like a marginal improvement, but you have to consider the fact that JSON is JavaScript object literal format. This means that by deserializing Protobuf in JavaScript, we have to convert binary to JSON in order to access the data in our code. And even with that conversion overhead, Protobuf manages to be faster than parsing JSON directly.

This shows that, in JavaScript (JS), even with the overhead of having to transform binary to JSON, Protobuf performs better than JSON itself.

Be aware that, for every implementation, you will have different numbers. Some are more optimized than others. However, a lot of implementations are just wrappers around the C implementation, which means you will get quasi-consistent deserialization.

Finally, it is important to mention that serialization and deserialization speeds depend a lot on the underlying data. Some data formats perform better on certain kinds of data. So, if you are considering using any data schema, I urge you to do some benchmarking first. It will prevent you from being surprised.

Readability of data

As you might expect, readability of data is not where Protobuf shines. As the serialized data is in binary, it requires more effort or tools for humans to be able to understand it. Let's take a look at the following hexadecimal:

```
0a 07 43 6c 65 6d 65 6e 74 10 64 1a 06 0a 04 4d 61 72 6b 1a 06 0a 04
4a 6f 68 6e
```

We have no way to guess that the preceding hexadecimal represents a `Person` object.

Now, while the default way of serializing data is not human-readable, Protobuf provides libraries to serialize data into JSON or the Protobuf text format. We can take the previous data that we had in hexadecimal and get text output similar to that in the following (Protobuf text format) code block:

```
name: "Clément"
age: 100
friends: {
  name: "Mark"
}
friends: {
  name: "John"
}
```

Furthermore, this text format can also be used to create binary. This means that we could have a configuration file written in text and still use the data with Protobuf.

So, as we saw, Protobuf serialized data is by default not human-readable. It is binary and it would take some extra effort or more tools to read. However, since Protobuf provides a way to serialize data to its own text format or to JSON, we can still have human-readable serialized data. This is nice for configuration files, test data, and so on.

Type safety

An advantage that schema-backed data formats have is that the schemas are generally defined with types in mind. Protobuf can define objects called messages that contain fields that are themselves typed. We saw a few examples previously in this chapter. This means that we will be able to check at compile time that the values provided for certain fields are correct.

On top of that, since Protobuf has an extensive set of types, there is the possibility to optimize for specific use cases. An example of this is the type for the age field that we saw in Person. In JSON Schema, for example, we would have a type called integer; however, this does not ensure that we do not provide negative numbers. In Protobuf, we could use uint32 (unsigned 32-bit integer) or a uint64 (usigned 64-bit integer) and thus we would, at compile time, ensure that we do not get negative numbers.

Finally, Protobuf also provides the possibility to nest types and reference these types by their fully qualified name. This basically means that the types have scopes. Let us take an example to make things clearer. Let us say that we have the following definitions (note that this is simplified):

```
message PhoneNumber {
    enum Type {
        Mobile,
        Work,
        Fax
    }

    Type type;
    string number;
}

message Email {
    enum Type {
        Personal,
        Work
    }

    Type type;
    string email;
}
```

As we can see, we defined two enums called Type. It is necessary because PhoneNumber supports Fax and Mobile but Email does not. Now, here when we are dealing with the Type enum in PhoneNumber, we are going to refer to it as PhoneNumber.Type, and when we deal with the one in Email, we will refer to it as Email.Type. These names are the fully qualified names of the types and they differentiate the two types, which have the same name, by providing a scope.

Now, let us think about what would happen if we had the following definitions:

```
enum Type {
    Mobile,
    Work,
    Fax,
    Personal
}
```

```
  }

  message PhoneNumber {
    Type type;
    string number;
  }

  message Email {
    Type type;
    string email;
  }
```

We could still create valid `Email` instances and `PhoneNumber` instances because we have all the types in the `Type` enum. However, in this case, we could also create invalid `Emails` and `PhoneNumbers`. For example, it is possible to create an `Email` type with the `Mobile` type. This means that by providing scoping for types, we can have type safety without having to create two enums:

```
  enum PhoneType { /*...*/ }
  enum EmailType { /*...*/ }
```

This is verbose and unnecessary since Protobuf lets us create types that will be called `Phone.Type` and `Email.Type`.

To summarize, Protobuf lets us use types in a very explicit and safe way. We have an extensive set of types that we can use and that will let us ensure that our data is correct at compile time. Finally, we saw that by providing nested types referenced by their fully qualified names, we can differentiate types with the same names and ensure that only certain correct values get set to fields.

Readability of schema

Finally, Protobuf has readable schemas because it was designed as self-documenting and as a language. We can find a lot of concepts that we are already familiar with such as type, comments, and imports. All of this makes onboarding new developers and using Protobuf-backed APIs easy.

The first thing worth mentioning is that we can have comments in our schemas to describe what the fields and types are doing. One of the best examples of that is in the proto files provided in Protobuf itself. Let's look at `duration.proto` (simplified for brevity) in the following code block:

```
  // A Duration represents a signed, fixed-length span of time
  represented
  // as a count of seconds and fractions of seconds at nanosecond
  // resolution. It is independent of any calendar and concepts like
  "day" or "month".
  message Duration {
    // Signed seconds of the span of time. Must be from -315,576,000,000
```

```
    // to +315,576,000,000 inclusive. Note: these bounds are computed
from:
    // 60 sec/min * 60 min/hr * 24 hr/day * 365.25 days/year * 10000
    years
    int64 seconds;

    // Signed fractions of a second at nanosecond resolution of the span
    // of time. Durations less than one second are represented with a 0
    // `seconds` field and a positive or negative `nanos` field. For
    durations
    // of one second or more, a non-zero value for the `nanos` field
    must be
    // of the same sign as the `seconds` field. Must be from
    -999,999,999
    // to +999,999,999 inclusive.
    int32 nanos;
}
```

We can see that we have a comment explaining the purpose of Duration and two others explaining what the fields represent, what their possible values are, and so on. This is important because it helps users use the types properly and it can let us make assumptions.

Next, we can import some other schema files to reuse types. This helps a lot, especially when the project becomes bigger. Instead of having to duplicate code or write everything in one file, we can separate by concern and reuse definitions in multiple places. Furthermore, since imports use the path of the schema file to access the definition in it, we can look at the definition. Now, this requires knowing a little bit more about the compiler and its options, but other than that, we can access the code and start poking around.

Finally, as we mentioned earlier, Protobuf has explicit typing. By looking at a field, we know exactly what kind of value we need to set and what the boundaries are (if any). Furthermore, after learning a little bit about the internals of serialization in Protobuf, you will be able to optimize the types that you use in a granular way.

Summary

In this chapter, we defined what serialization and deserialization are, we saw the goals we try to achieve with them, and we talked about where Protobuf stands. We saw that there are a lot of trade-offs when choosing a data format that fulfills all the requirements. We also saw that, in serialization, we do not only care about one criterion; rather, there are many criteria that we need to look at. And finally, we saw the advantages and disadvantages of Protobuf as a data format.

In the next chapter, we will talk about the Protobuf language and all its concepts. We will see how to define types, import other schemas, and other language concepts.

Quiz

1. Serialization **to file** is the action of taking data from ___ memory and putting it in ___ memory.

    A. Non-volatile, volatile

    B. Volatile, non-volatile

2. Deserialization **from file** is the action of taking data from ___ memory and putting it in ___ memory.

    A. Non-volatile, volatile

    B. Volatile, non-volatile

3. What is availability in the context of serialization and deserialization?

    A. The time it takes for deserialization to make the data available in your code

    B. The time it takes for serialization to make the data available in a file

    C. None of the above

4. When is serialized data considered human-readable?

    A. If we can, by any means, decode the data

    B. If a machine can easily read it

    C. If humans can easily understand the structure of the data

Answers

1. B

2. A

3. A

4. C

2
Protobuf is a Language

It is time to discover the Protobuf language and its syntax. In this chapter, we are going to see all the concepts that we need in order to write Protobuf schemas. This chapter is, thus, designed as a kind of documentation that can be read from start to end but also can be referenced in future chapters. As such, you might not understand every implication of each concept, but that is fine. Be confident, and we will make sure that you get all the knowledge you need throughout this book.

In this chapter, we will learn about the following:

- Top-level statements
- User-defined types
- Out-of-the-box types
- Services

At the end of this chapter, you will know all the most common concepts in the Protobuf language. You will understand what they are used for, and you will be able to start writing proto files.

Technical requirements

All the code examples that you will see in this section can be found under the directory called `chapter2` in the GitHub repository (`https://github.com/PacktPublishing/Protocol-Buffers-Handbook`).

In the following sections, I will be using some **extended Backus-Naur form** (**EBNF**) notation (`https://en.wikipedia.org/wiki/Extended_Backus%E2%80%93Naur_form`) to describe the syntax of all the elements. The following elements will be used:

```
|    alternation (or)
()   grouping
[]   option (zero or one time)
{}   repetition (any number of times)
```

Do not worry too much, though. I am only writing in the EBNF for people who are interested and to emphasize that Protobuf is a language. If you feel like this is too overwhelming, you can just skip this part and look at the examples I will be providing.

On top of that, I will be omitting details for simplicity. However, all the details are available in the official specifications:

- proto2: `https://protobuf.dev/reference/protobuf/proto2-spec`

- proto3: `https://protobuf.dev/reference/protobuf/proto3-spec`

Top-level statements

In this section, we will see all the top-level statements in the order they should appear in a proto file according to the *Protobuf Style Guide* (`https://protobuf.dev/programming-guides/style/`). We are going to go through their meaning, and we are going to see some simple examples.

Syntax

The syntax statement is one of the easiest statements to understand. This tells the compiler (protoc) the version we are using in the file and, therefore, the features we can and cannot access:

EBNF – Syntax statement

```
version = "proto2" | "proto3" | "editions"
syntax = "syntax" "=" ("'" version "'" | '"' version '"') ";"
```

As you can see, there are three versions that we can pass to the syntax statement:

- proto2

- proto3

- editions

Now, all of this is a little bit obscure, and these names, especially `proto2` and `proto3`, are misnomers. `proto3` is not really a better version than `proto2`; they just provide different features. For example, the internals of Protobuf are written in `proto2`, and most of the code written outside of Protobuf is written in `proto3`.

To solve this misnomer problem, the Protobuf team is working on adding editions. The goal of the edition is to let the language evolve over time without having to release full versions each time. The Protobuf team will be able to ameliorate Protobuf step by step, and you will have the choice of features you want to enable/disable.

Edition

As we mentioned previously in the syntax subsection, editions will provide more flexibility to the language. We will be able to roll out ameliorations step by step by simply incrementing our version in the edition statement:

EBNF – Edition statement

```
version = "2023" | "2024" | ...
edition = "edition" "=" ("'" version "'" | '"' version '"') ";"
```

Now, it is important to note that the version mentioned in the EBNF syntax is different than the previous version we defined. The Protobuf team chose to make editions named after the year they were released (e.g., 2023, 2024, etc.).

Package

Protobuf lets us define units of related schemas with packages. This can be useful for separating concerns and adding an extra layer of type safety:

EBNF– Package statement

```
ident = letter { letter | decimalDigit | "_" }
fullIdent = ident { "." ident }
package = "package" fullIdent ";"
```

As you can see in the syntax, packages accept a fully qualified identifier. This means that the following are the correct names:

- `google`
- `google.protobuf`
- `google.protobuf.v2`

With these names, we can reference the definitions in them by prepending the name of the package to the type. If we have a message called Person living under the package packt.protobuf.ch2, we could reference it by writing packt.protobuf.ch2.Person from outside the package, or Person if we were referencing it from within the packt.protobuf.ch2 package.

Import

Protobuf, like a lot of other languages, lets us split source code into multiple files to increase reusability:

EBNF – Import statement

```
import = "import" [ "weak" | "public" ] pathAsString ";"
```

The most common example of reusability is using the well-known types already provided in Protobuf (more on that in the "Out-of-the-box types" section). For example, we can use the Duration type by importing the duration.proto file:

```
import "google/protobuf/duration.proto";
```

Then, because the Duration type is defined under the google.protobuf package, we can use the type by writing google.protobuf.Duration.

Now, if you come from an object-oriented language background, you might have heard of "creating a file per class." While you might be tempted to do that with Protobuf, the recommendation is to keep all the relevant definitions together and split the definitions that can be reused separately. duration.proto is such an example of splitting the definitions to increase reusability. In this case, we want to only import Duration and reuse it in multiple places.

Finally, you can notice the two keywords: weak and public. I added weak for the sake of completeness, but this is only used internally at Google. So, let us forget about this one. However, public is interesting since it lets you create transitive dependencies. This means that if a.proto imports b.proto publicly, any proto file importing a.proto will also have access to the definitions in b.proto.

Option

Options, or FileOptions (see `https://github.com/protocolbuffers/protobuf/blob/main/src/google/protobuf/descriptor.proto`), are the concepts we can use to influence the code generated by the compiler (protoc). We will discuss this and see some examples in this book, but right now, we can just understand options as being the metadata needed for the compilation of our proto files:

EBNF – Option statement

```
optionName = ( ident | "(" ["."] fullIdent ")" )
option = "option" optionName  "=" constant ";"
```

An example of this is the `option` called deprecated, which, depending on the programming language you are using, will mark all the types in the file as deprecated. Here is what it looks like:

```
option deprecated = true;
```

It is also possible to define custom options, and this is why we can use full identifiers as option names. These custom options can then be used by protoc plugins or other tools. We are going to discuss how to do this in *Chapter 9* of this book, and we will implement a protoc plugin that will look for the custom option we define.

Finally, you can see in the syntax that we are passing constants to options. These constants can get quite complex, but for now, you can just think of them as `booleans`, `strings`, `floats`, `integers`, and `identifiers`. In *Chapter 9*, we will see that they can also take messages as values.

User-defined types

enum

You are certainly already familiar with enums in your favorite language, and they are pretty much the same in Protobuf. When we know all the possible values of a type, we use enums to create a lightweight representation of each value:

EBNF – Enum syntax

```
enumValueOption = optionName "=" constant
enumField = ident "=" [ "-" ] intLit [ "[" enumValueOption {
"," enumValueOption } "]" ];"
enumBody = "{" { option | enumField | reserved } "}"
enum = "enum" ident enumBody
```

As such, an enum in Protobuf looks like the following:

```
enum PhoneType {
    PHONE_TYPE_MOBILE = 0;
    PHONE_TYPE_HOME = 1;
    //...
}
```

You can see that we are adding the name of the enum (in UPPER_SNAKE_CASE) as the prefix of each value, and then we have this magic number following the equal sign. The naming is purely done according to convention (recommended in the *Protobuf Style Guide*). As for the magic number, which is called a tag, for now, you can just see this number as the value that will be encoded. This is not entirely true, and we will see why when we talk about these numbers in the message fields.

Now, the main difference between enums in proto2 and proto3 is that enums in proto3 are open. An open enum is an enum that does not reject values that are not defined. Let us take the example of setting a field with the type PhoneType to a value of 3. In proto2, it would simply be impossible to do so because the compiler would refuse such a value. However, the proto3 compiler would accept the value.

This is why, in proto3, it is recommended to add an UNSPECIFIED value with the 0 tag in every enum. Here is what it looks like:

```
enum PhoneType {
    PHONE_TYPE_UNSPECIFIED = 0;
    PHONE_TYPE_MOBILE = 1;
    PHONE_TYPE_HOME = 2;
    //...
}
```

Any value not defined in this enum will be attributed to the UNSPECIFIED value at deserialization time. This means that, in the case of the value 3, we are going to serialize 3, and when deserializing the field, it will be marked as unset, and, thus, Protobuf will assign the default value to your field, which is zero (UNSPECIFIED) for enums. We will see more about defaults in the message fields.

Finally, as you can see in the syntax, we can use options in the enum body (EnumOptions) and on every value (EnumValueOptions). As for FileOptions, they are also available in the descriptor. proto (check https://github.com/protocolbuffers/protobuf/blob/main/src/google/protobuf/descriptor.proto) file. I will let you check all the options for yourself, but let us write an example of how to use them.

For options in the enum body, this is very similar to options at the file level. It looks like this:

```
enum OldPhoneType {
    option deprecated = true;
```

```
//...
}
```

For the value options, they are a little bit different. We write them between square braces ([ ]) and separate them with commas. It looks like this:

```
enum PhoneType {
  //...
  // disclosure: description is a custom option!
  PHONE_TYPE_FAX = 3 [deprecated = true, description = "who uses fax
  machines anymore?"];
}
```

Finally, in the syntax, you can find `reserved`. We will be talking about that when we talk about messages because we need to learn about the concept of field tags first.

Message

Messages are the most complex concept in Protobuf. This is why we are going to split this section into multiple subsections. We will talk about these concepts in the following order:

- Options: They are repeated in all the following concepts
- Field, reserved, map, and oneof: These concepts are all about defining fields and specifying some serialization behavior
- Nested messages

EBNF – Message syntax

```
messageBody = "{" { field | enum | message | option | oneof | mapField
| reserved } "}"
message = "message" ident messageBody
```

Option

Since we are already familiar with options at this point, we can skip them. However, I still want to mention all the types that you can look for in the descriptor.proto (check `https://github.com/protocolbuffers/protobuf/blob/main/src/google/protobuf/descriptor.proto`) file so that you can check all the possible options available. Here is the list per concept:

`message -> MessageOptions`

`enum -> EnumOptions`

`field/mapField -> FieldOptions`

```
oneof -> OneofOptions
```

I highly recommend you check the definitions since it will help you read more Protobuf code. However, you might prefer finishing this section first because these types are defined as messages.

Field

A message is mainly a collection of fields. They represent the actual data to be serialized and deserialized:

EBNF – Field syntax

```
label = "required" | "optional" | "repeated"
type = "double" | "float" | "int32" | "int64" | "uint32" | "uint64" |
"sint32" | "sint64" | "fixed32" | "fixed64" | "sfixed32" | "sfixed64"
| "bool" | "string" | "bytes" | messageType | enumType
fieldOption = optionName "=" constant
field = label type ident "=" intLit [ "[" fieldOption {
"," fieldOption } "]" ] ";"
```

To write a field, we write one of the types available, the name of the field, and then we assign a tag (remember the magic number we saw in enums?). This can look like this:

```
bool is_authenticated = 1;
```

Now, in the case of fields, the main difference that you have between proto2 and proto3 is the fact that in proto2, you can have the labels required and optional in front of the field. In proto3, every field is optional by default. This means that we can set a value (or not) in a field, whereas in proto2, having a required field without a value would not compile.

You might be thinking that having the required and optional keywords is helpful and more explicit. If so, you would not be alone. A lot of questions around proto3 are about making sure that the field has a value set to it, and this is tricky because fields in proto3 have default values. Here is the list of defaults per type:

```
"double" | "float" | "int32" | "int64" | "uint32" | "uint64" |
"sint32" | "sint64" | "fixed32" | "fixed64" | "sfixed32" | "sfixed64"
| enumType -> 0
"bool" -> false
"string" | "bytes" -> empty array of char/byte
messageType -> empty message
```

You might ask yourself, how do I distinguish between the default value and a value that I set? If I set 0 to an `int32` field, is there a way to find whether I set it or if it is the default value? It turns out you can. Protobuf will generate some code you can call to check if the field is set or not. If you want more information on this, consider checking the following documentation: `https://github.com/protocolbuffers/protobuf/blob/main/docs/field_presence.md`.

Next, there is the third label called `repeated`. This is a label that we can use in both versions. It means that the field is a list of the following type (this defaults to an empty list if not set). For example, if we wanted to have a person with multiple middle names, we could use the following:

```
repeated string middle_names = 1;
```

Notice that if we follow the *Protobuf Style Guide*, we should pluralize the name of the repeated fields. In that case, we have middle_names, not middle_name.

Finally, fields have tags. During the `enum` section, we said that these are the values to which the `enum` values will be serialized. While this is partially true for enums, this is not true for fields in messages. Tags are numerical identifiers for fields. When we write something like the following:

```
int32 age = 1;
```

it does not mean we are setting the value 1 to age; it means we set the identifier for this field to 1. This is how Protobuf knows where to deserialize data. Protobuf will serialize data to binary in the following format:

```
(id + type) value
```

Right now, it is not important to understand the internals of serialization, but what you need to understand is that these tags are what will be serialized (not the field names), and Protobuf will use that to populate the fields according to the tag value. In *Chapter 5*, we will come back to this to see how Protobuf serializes the data in more detail.

Reserved

Since we learned about fields, we will go through a more complex concept, which is reserving tags and field names. We will not go into details about why this is useful yet (more about that in *Chapter 6*), but we will see the basics.

Reserving a field tag and/or a field name makes the `reserved` element not usable anymore:

EBNF – Reserved syntax

```
ranges = range { "," range }
range =  intLit [ "to" ( intLit | "max" ) ]
strFieldNames = strFieldName { "," strFieldName }
```

```
strFieldName = "'" fieldName "'" | '"' fieldName '"'
reserved = "reserved" ( ranges | strFieldNames ) ";"
```

This means that the following code,

```
message InvalidField {
   reserved 1;
   uint32 id = 1;
}
```

will not compile because we reserved the tag 1. Similarly,

```
message InvalidField {
   reserved "id";
   uint32 id = 1;
}
```

will not compile because we reserved the name id.

Another thing to mention is that we can define more complex ranges of tags. If we wanted to remove the tags from 1 to 10, we would write the following:

```
reserved 1 to 10;
```

The start and the end of the range are inclusive. Meaning that we reserved the tag from 1 to 10 and not from 1 to 9.

We could also exclude a wider range of tags:

```
reserved 1 to max;
```

In this case, we reserved all the possible tags. This is obviously not useful because it would mean we cannot define any field in the message. I just wanted to show you that you can use the max keyword at the end of the range.

Now, since this is pretty early in this book, and I do not want to make you too afraid, the most important thing you need to remember here is that we make sure that other people do not use a certain field tag/name. If you are curious about why you would need that, I invite you to go to *Chapter 6*.

MapField

On top of scalar fields and lists (repeated), we can also have maps. You might already be familiar with the concept of a map (also named dictionary), but to summarize, we create key-value relationships so that, later, we can find the value by searching for the key:

EBNF – Map syntax

```
keyType = "int32" | "int64" | "uint32" | "uint64" | "sint32" |
"sint64" | "fixed32" | "fixed64" | "sfixed32" | "sfixed64" | "bool" |
"string"
mapField = "map" "<" keyType "," type ">" ident "=" intLit [ "["
fieldOptions "]" ] ";"
```

In Protobuf, we can write a map like this:

```
map<string, int32> occurrences = 1;
```

Notice that not all the types we saw previously in the field subsection are available as key types. We cannot use float/double, bytes, or message types as key types. Other than that restriction, as you can see, maps are similar to fields.

Oneof

Sometimes, we need to explicitly set one value or the other. This kind of mutually exclusive data can be defined with oneof fields. They wrap multiple fields and enforce the logic of only one of those fields having a value.

EBNF – oneof syntax

```
oneofField = type ident "=" intLit [ "[" fieldOptions "]" ] ";"
oneof = "oneof" ident "{" { option | oneofField } "}"
```

We can be define oneof like this:

```
oneof result {
  Success success = 1;
  Error error = 2;
}
```

One important thing to note for oneofs is that they can sometimes be replaced by enums and for reasons that we are going to see in *Chapter 5*, it is better to do so. oneofs can be replaced by enums when the field types are very simple, such as with bool, and if we know all the possible values. For example, if we had:

```
oneof book_type {
  bool paperback = 1;
  bool ebook = 2;
  bool audiobook = 3;
}
```

We could just replace this with:

```
enum BookType {
  BOOK_TYPE_UNSPECIFIED = 0;
  BOOK_TYPE_PAPERBACK = 1;
  BOOK_TYPE_EBOOK = 2;
  BOOK_TYPE_AUDIOBOOK = 3;
}
```

However, if we were dealing with more complex types, such as:

```
message PaperBack { /*...*/ }
message Ebook { /*...*/ }
message AudioBook { /*...*/ }
//...
oneof book_type {
  PaperBack paperback = 1;
  Ebook ebook = 2;
  AudioBook audiobook = 3;
}
```

We wouldn't be able to transform that into an enum because Paperback, Ebook, and AudioBook might have extra information defined inside them that we cannot replicate with a simple enum.

Message

You might be wondering why I decided to talk about nested messages and not about nested enums. In fact, the syntax for both nested messages and enums is exactly the same if they are at the top level or nested inside a message. The main thing to note for nested messages is that we have a limit for nesting. We can have a maximum of 31 nested messages.

Now, please understand that this is generally not what you want. In Protobuf, we try to keep the nesting as low as possible. The maximum nesting that can be found in the internals of Protobuf is 1, meaning one nested message into another.

Nested messages provide specialization in terms of messages. Here's an example:

```
message Cat {
  enum Breed {
    BREED_UNSPECIFIED = 0;
    BREED_SIAMESE = 1;
    BREED_PERSIAN = 2;
    //...
  }
}
message Dog {
  enum Breed {
    BREED_UNSPECIFIED = 0;
    BREED_GERMAN_SHEPERD = 1;
    BREED_BULLDOG = 2;
    //...
  }
}
```

This can help us make our program more type-safe by making sure that the Breed is specific to the animal in question and that, for example, we cannot set the value GERMAN_SHEPERD to cat. In this case, we will be more explicit about what Breed we are talking about by using the fully qualified name: Dog.Breed and Cat.Breed.

Finally, another use case for nesting is if the nested message is only relevant in the context of the parent message and cannot be reused in other objects. An example of this can be seen in the following:

```
message Address {
  message Building {
    message Apartment {
      /*...*/
    }
  }
}
```

Here, an Apartment is only relevant in the Building context, and the Building is only relevant in the Address context. We do not want to expose these types outside of these contexts, and we want to make sure that when a developer uses these types, the context is clear. The developer will only be able to use these types with their fully qualified names (e.g., Address.Building.Apartment), and, thus, it might make them think twice before using it for something unrelated.

Services

Finally, the last concept we are going to see is `service`. `service` is designed for Protobuf interaction with RPC frameworks, such as gRPC. They define a type-safe contract that the server should implement and that the client can call:

EBNF – Service syntax

```
rpc = "rpc" ident "(" [ "stream" ] messageType ")" "returns" "(" [
"stream" ] messageType ")" (( "{" option "}" ) | ";")
service = "service" ident "{" { option | rpc } "}"
```

For example, we could have the following `service`:

```
service BookService {
  rpc ListBooks(ListBooksRequest) returns (ListBooksResponse);
  rpc GetBook(GetBookRequest) returns (Book);
  rpc CreateBook(CreateBookRequest) returns (Book);
  rpc UpdateBook(UpdateBookRequest) returns (Book);
  rpc DeleteBook(DeleteBookRequest) returns (google.protobuf.Empty);
}
```

It defines a contract for the `BookService`. The server will implement the `List`, `Get`, `Create`, `Update`, and `Delete` operations. Each of them will take some data as input (the types ending with `Request`) and will return some data as output (`ListBooksResponse`, `Book`, and `google.protobuf.Empty`). The client will also be aware of these parameters and outputs so that they can create requests and get responses back from the server.

Now, all of this is not relevant in the context of Protobuf itself. These services are only here for RPC frameworks to define contracts. In this book, we will not talk about them anymore since they are not related to serialization, but you can check out `grpc.io` to see how to use them in your favorite language.

Out-of-the-box types

On top of all the scalar types that Protobuf provides as part of the language, it also provides some already-defined types called **well-known types (WKTs)**. All these types can be found in the `src/google/protobuf` folder in the GitHub repository (`https://github.com/protocolbuffers/protobuf/tree/main/src/google/protobuf`), and they are all defined under the `google.protobuf` package.

Here is a list of the most common WKTs available:

- `Duration`
- `Timestamp`

- FieldMask

- Any

- Struct

Let's go through all of these types and see what they are used for.

Duration and timestamp

These two types are pretty interesting because they show us the importance of naming, documenting with comments, and separating definitions into different files for reusability. In fact, these two types have the same definitions except for the message name. Here are the `diff` command results between those two (simplified):

```
-message Timestamp {
-   // Represents seconds of UTC time since Unix epoch
-   // 1970-01-01T00:00:00Z. Must be from 0001-01-01T00:00:00Z to
-   // 9999-12-31T23:59:59Z inclusive.
+message Duration {
+   // Signed seconds of the span of time. Must be from
-315,576,000,000
+   // to +315,576,000,000 inclusive. Note: these bounds are computed
from:
+   // 60 sec/min * 60 min/hr * 24 hr/day * 365.25 days/year * 10000
years
    int64 seconds = 1;


-   // Non-negative fractions of a second at nanosecond resolution.
Negative
-   // second values with fractions must still have non-negative nanos
values
-   // that count forward in time. Must be from 0 to 999,999,999
-   // inclusive.
+   // Signed fractions of a second at nanosecond resolution of the
span
+   // of time. Durations less than one second are represented with a 0
+   // `seconds` field and a positive or negative `nanos` field. For
durations
+   // of one second or more, a non-zero value for the `nanos` field
must be
+   // of the same sign as the `seconds` field. Must be from
-999,999,999
+   // to +999,999,999 inclusive.
    int32 nanos = 2;
}
```

You can see that the main things that changed are the name of the message and the comments on top of the fields. Otherwise, the fields are the same (seconds and nanos).

These two types, as their names suggest, differ only in meaning. In Protobuf, Timestamp is described as representing "a point in time," and Duration is described as representing "a span of time." This means that if we needed information about a point in time, such as with an updated_at field in an account, we would use Timestamp. If we needed information about some span of time, such as the length of a running race, we would use Duration.

Finally, here is how you can use these types:

```
import "google/protobuf/duration.proto";
import "google/protobuf/timestamp.proto";

message RunRace {
  google.protobuf.Duration length = 1;
}

message Account {
  google.protobuf.Timestamp updated_at = 1;
}
```

We first import the relevant WKT proto files, and then we reference the types with their fully qualified names.

FieldMask

Sometimes, we need a way to select a subset of fields for a given message. Generally, this is done to reduce the payload size and make serialization/deserialization faster. We can do so with the use of FieldMasks. These masks help us define a list of "paths" that we want to keep. Here is the definition of FieldMask (simplified):

```
message FieldMask {
  repeated string paths = 1;
}
```

The paths represent how to access a certain piece of data. For a simple message, such as:

```
message Account {
  User user = 1;
  Photo photo = 2;
}
```

if we wanted to keep only the user information, we would use the `user` path. Now, this gets a little bit longer if we want to keep only the user's name. If we have the user message as:

```
message User {
  string name = 1;
  //...
}
```

then we will have the path `user.name`. Once we apply this mask to the `Account` type, we will only get the user name field set.

Now, the main reason for using `FieldMask` is that after applying it to an object (e.g., `Account`), we will see all the other fields cleared out, and we can only serialize the information needed. This is because unset fields do not create size overhead in serialization. In our example, we would be serializing an `Account` object by only having the user's name.

Finally, note that `field` defined in `oneof` types is considered a field defined in the containing message. This means that when applying a `FieldMask` on a `oneof` field, you can directly use its name and not the name of `oneof` followed by the field name. Here is an example:

```
message Book {
  oneof book_type {
    PaperBack paperback = 1;
    Ebook ebook = 2;
    AudioBook audiobook = 3;
  }
}
```

If we only care about the paperback information, we would have the `paperback` path directly, not `book_type.paperback`.

Any

As its name suggests, Any can represent any Protobuf message. We can serialize a message and keep the raw bytes inside it. This is basically a dynamic object.

The Any definition looks like this (simplified):

```
message Any {
  string type_url = 1;
  bytes value = 2;
}
```

Let's not worry too much about the `type_url` field. This is just a unique identifier that tells which type the underlying bytes are corresponding to. Then, we have the value field, which is of the `bytes` type. This represents a serialized message. As we know, Protobuf serializes data to binary, and thus, we can simply put this binary into the value field.

Once an `Any` instance is created (the operation is called packing), we can retrieve the underlying data and populate an object out of it depending on the `type_url` (the operation is called unpacking).

Struct

The last common WKT is `Struct`. This one also represents a dynamic object but in a way that is similar to what the JSON format is doing. The definition of `Struct` looks like the following (simplified):

```
message Struct {
    map<string, Value> fields = 1;
}

message Value {
    oneof kind {
        NullValue null_value = 1;
        double number_value = 2;
        string string_value = 3;
        bool bool_value = 4;
        Struct struct_value = 5;
        ListValue list_value = 6;
    }
}
enum NullValue {
    NULL_VALUE = 0;
}
message ListValue {
    repeated Value values = 1;
}
```

As you can see, this example uses a little bit of everything that we have learned so far: messages, oneofs, fields, enums, repeated fields, and maps.

Now, you can notice that `Struct` is really just a map. So, we basically have a key-value pair. That is why I said `Struct` is similar to a JSON object. Other than that, I believe that with the Protobuf reading skills you have now, the rest should not be a problem for you.

Summary

We have come a long way. This chapter was intense, and there are probably things that you are still not entirely sure about. That is normal; do not worry. You can refer to it later if you have questions about a certain Protobuf concept.

In this chapter, we saw how to write top-level statements such as Edition, Syntax, Import, Package, and Options. We then saw how to write enums and messages to create type definitions. After that, we saw what the services are. Finally, we talked about the well-known types that are provided out of the box when you use Protobuf.

In the next chapter, we will talk about the Protobuf text format and how we can set values to fields in a nonprogrammatic way.

Quiz

1. Where can you find the proto files for the well-known types?

   A. Nowhere; this is hidden inside the Protobuf language.

   B. Nowhere; we need to define them ourselves.

   C. On the GitHub repository under the src/google/protobuf folder.

2. Where can you find the message definitions for the option types?

   A. On the GitHub repository under the folder src/google/protobuf in the file called descriptor.proto.

   B. Nowhere; this is hidden inside the Protobuf language.

   C. Nowhere; we need to define them ourselves.

3. Why do we define an UNSPECIFIED value in enums for proto3?

   A. In proto3, enums are closed, so we do not need to.

   B. In proto3, enums are open, and UNSPECIFIED is used as the default value.

   C. It is not needed in proto3, only in proto2.

4. When do we need nesting types inside a message?

   A. When we want to specialize a type with fully qualified names.

   B. When a type is only relevant in the parent context.

   C. All the above.

Answers

1. C
2. A
3. B
4. C

3

Describing Data with Protobuf Text Format

Before moving towards learning the internals of Protobuf, there is another skill that we need to learn. This skill is reading and writing `txtpb` files. They contain data written in the Protobuf text format, which is the text representation of the data that we deserialize from the binary form or the data that we want to serialize into binary form.

In this chapter, we're going to cover the following main topics:

- Why use the text format
- Writing scalar values
- Writing complex types

At the end of this chapter, you will know what the Protobuf text format is and what it is used for. However, most importantly, you will be able to write data that we will later use to discover the internals of serialization and deserialization.

Technical requirements

All the code examples that you will see in this section can be found under the directory called `chapter3` in the GitHub repository here: (`https://github.com/PacktPublishing/Protocol-Buffers-Handbook`).

Why use the text format?

During the primer on serialization, we said that the main reason for using Protobuf is that it reduces the payload by serializing to binary. But remember that we also said that the very binary that saves us a lot of bandwidth can cost us in terms of readability. This is because it would take way more human effort to read the binary than to read the text directly.

To solve this problem, Protobuf can also serialize data to text. It can serialize data to JSON, for example, but for this book, the most interesting text format that it can serialize to is its own text format. There are several advantages to this text format, but let us first describe what the use cases are for having a text representation of your data.

The most obvious use case is for debugging. This is a stressful and not-so-enjoyable part of our job. We do not want to add extra complexity on top of the already complex process. As such, we try to make each payload clear by making them readable with something like the following:

```
id: "a_unique_id"
label: "Total Amount"
quantity: 1
amount {
  currency_code: "USD"
  units: 9
  nanos: 990000000
}
```

This is much easier to debug than something like this:

```
0a 0b 61 5f 75 6e 69 71   75 65 5f 69 64 12 0c 54
6f 74 61 6c 20 41 6d 6f   75 6e 74 18 01 22 0d 0a
03 55 53 44 10 09 18 80   e7 88 d8 03
```

In the text representation, we can clearly read every field and the corresponding data, whereas in the binary, we would have to figure out what the field metadata and the actual data are.

Another use case in which the Protobuf text format is useful is for configuration. Since humans are the main readers and editors of configuration files, we need to have some textual representation of the data. On top of the other benefits that we mentioned during the first use case, there are a few others:

- There are fewer boilerplate characters than in JSON or XML; thus, writing the configuration file is faster.

- At the time of serialization, Protobuf will check the types for each and every field. If a developer sets the wrong data to a field, Protobuf will let you know.

- We can add comments and headers to give extra information to developers.

Less boilerplate

The Protobuf text format is similar to JSON. However, as we saw in the example above, it feels less cluttered with unnecessary characters. The equivalent JSON to the txtpb, which we saw previously, would look like the following:

```
{
    "id": "a_unique_id",
    "label": "Total Amount",
    "quantity": 1,
    "amount": {
      "currency_code": "USD",
      "units": 9,
      "nanos": 990000000
    }
}
```

In total, such a JSON file is 157 bytes, whereas the equivalent `txtpb` file is 116 bytes. But more importantly, it is easier to write the txtpb file for the following reasons:

- There are no outer braces for the first level
- There are no commas between the fields
- The keys are not enclosed by double quotes
- You can omit colons when defining a field that uses a user-defined type (see amount)

In the end, I believe that we can agree on the fact that we use fewer keystrokes to write a txtpb file and that, obviously, it takes less space on disk to store such a file. This makes this format easy to write and read because it is less cluttered.

Type safety

As we know, Protobuf is designed to be type-safe. This means that if we passed the wrong value to a txtpb file and tried to serialize/deserialize it, Protobuf would give us messages like the following (set "9" string to integer field):

```
Providing "9" instead of 9 to units field: Expected integer, got: "9"
```

This is especially useful to catch errors before it is too late. If we had a configuration file with an invalid value, we would be able to catch the configuration at the entry point of our application and not later during runtime. This reduces the feedback loop for developers, and it costs less resources to fix the bug than if we had to redeploy.

Headers and comments

Finally, we can have comments right next to the data. This means that we can explain what the field is doing or even add some "metadata" at the beginning of the file. For example, we can add headers that would be used by a tool or developers to understand them. The text format specification displays the following example:

```
# proto-file: some/proto/my_file.proto
# proto-message: MyMessage
```

This shows us that the following data are supposed to be serialized using the message definition called `MyMessage`, and that the definition of that message is in the file `some/proto/my_file.proto`.

On top of these headers, we can add comments to fields. You might have noticed the weird `nanos` field in our previous txtpb example. If you did not read the definition code, which contains comments, you would have no way to guess what it means. Furthermore, even if the developer had the headers to be able to track down the definition, we can save some time by adding a comment right next to the field. This could look like the following:

```
amount {
  currency_code: "USD"
  units: 9 # 9 dollars
  nanos: 990000000 # 99 cents
}
```

This could also be used to warn the developers about some expectations around the value the field should have.

Finally, it is important to mention that these comments are not encoded into binary in any way. They are only here for the reader of the file. This means that once the data are in binary, you will lose all this information, but this also means that your documentation does not impact your payload size.

Describing data

As we saw, the main purpose of the Protobuf text format is to describe data in a textual representation. In this section, we are going to see the EBNF syntax for each concept in the format. This will be a reference that is similar to what we did in *Chapter 2*. Similar to what we did there, some details will be omitted to make the whole thing more readable, but all these details can be found on the specification page here: (`https://protobuf.dev/reference/protobuf/textformat-spec/`).

Scalar values

The most important part of the text format is the definition of scalar values. We already saw some examples at the beginning of this chapter, but we are going to talk about some details here:

Code example 1 – Scalar field syntax

```
ScalarValue  = String
             | Float
             | Identifier
             | SignedIdentifier
             | DecSignedInteger
             | OctSignedInteger
             | HexSignedInteger
             | DecUnsignedInteger
             | OctUnsignedInteger
             | HexUnsignedInteger ;
ScalarList   = "[" [ ScalarValue { "," ScalarValue } ] "]" ;
ScalarField = Identifier ":" ( ScalarValue | ScalarList ) [ ";" | ","
] ;
```

As you can see, in the EBNF syntax, a scalar field represents both a "normal" field and a repeated field. For a field with a single value, we could have something like the following:

```
age: 42
```

For a repeated field, we could have the following:

```
middle_names: [ "james", "henry" ]
```

One more thing to mention with repeated fields is that you can also write middle names by repeating the field multiple times:

```
middle_names: "james"
middle_names: "henry"
```

Finally, you can see that the values can take a lot of forms. I will let you check the specifications by yourself to see how to write strings, floats, identifiers, and so on.

Messages

Sometimes, we also need to provide value for user-defined types. In *Chapter 2*, we saw that we can define messages and use the type as the field type. Naturally, the Protobuf text format allows us to define such kinds of data:

Code example 2 – Message syntax

```
MessageValue = "{" Message "}" | "<" Message ">" ;
MessageList = "[" [ MessageValue { "," MessageValue } ] "]" ;
MessageField = Identifier [ ":" ] ( MessageValue | MessageList ) [ ";"
| "," ];
Field = ScalarField | MessageField ;
Message = "{" Field "}" ;
```

As you can see in the syntax, a message can be defined by surrounding fields by braces ({ }) or angle brackets (<>). While the angle brackets are valid syntax, it is preferable to use brackets. Tools such as txtpbfmt (`https://github.com/protocolbuffers/txtpbfmt`), which format txtpb files, will rewrite angle brackets to brackets. This means that we should prefer to write the following:

```
person {
  age: 42
  middle_names: [ "james", "henry" ]
}
```

You can also see that messages can be used inside repeated fields. So, for example, if we had a repeated field of Person, we could have the following:

```
friends: [
  { age: 42 middle_names: [ "james", "henry" ] },
  { age: 24 middle_names ["henry", "james"] }
]
```

Notice that I did not use commas between fields; this is because they are optional. However, if you feel uncomfortable skipping them, you can also write a message like this:

```
{ age: 42, middle_names: [ "james", "henry" ] }
```

Finally, in *Chapter 2*, we saw that we can nest messages. This means that in Protobuf text format, you could write something like the following:

```
msg1 {
  msg2 {
    #...
```

```
    }
  }
```

You would be limited to 31 nested messages, the same as the proto file definition.

Maps

As we saw in *Chapter 2*, Protobuf lets us associate keys and values with maps. These maps are actually syntax sugar around a repeated field of `MapFieldEntry`. This is an internal message that looks like the following:

```
message MapFieldEntry {
  optional KeyType key = 1;
  optional ValueType value = 2;
}
```

If you forgot what the possible values for `KeyType` and `ValueType` are, I recommend you go back to *Chapter 2* and check the section on Maps. But the most important thing here is that the map is actually just a repeated field of messages, and we already know how to do that from the two previous subsections. We know that we can write a repeated field like this:

```
name: [ … ]
```

and we know that we can write message values like this:

```
{ … }
```

In the end, we just have to mix both syntaxes to have a map:

```
occurrences: [
  { key: "possible", value: 8 },
  { key: "values", value: 10 }
]
```

That is all. You only need to remember that maps are syntactic sugar around repeated fields of `MapFieldEntry`, and that `MapFieldEntry` has two fields called `key` and `value`.

Oneofs

Remember that in Protobuf we can also create mutually exclusive fields with `oneof` fblocks. This means that at any point in time, only one field from the `oneof` will be set. Knowing all of that, we can guess that oneofs are simply fields, and that Protobuf will either return an error if two fields are set or it will use the last value set.

In the case of `oneof` blocks, if you set two fields, the compiler will give you an error. Let us first check a valid example. We have the following definition in a proto file:

```
syntax = "proto3";

import "google/protobuf/duration.proto";

message AudioBook {
  google.protobuf.Duration duration = 1;
  //...
}

message HardCover {
  uint64 pages = 1;
  //...
}

message Book {
  oneof Type {
    AudioBook audio_book = 1;
    HardCover hard_cover = 2;
  }
}
```

Passing the following data is valid:

```
hard_cover {
  pages: 200
}
```

This is because we are only setting one field of the `oneof` inside book. Now, if we set both `audio_book` and `hard_cover`, like this:

```
hard_cover {
  pages: 200
}
audio_book {
  duration {
    seconds: 9000 # 2h30
  }
}
```

we would get the following error:

```
Field "audio_book" is specified along with field "hard_cover", another
member of oneof "Type".
```

In the end, these are mainly fields that have extra requirements to be mutually exclusive. We already know how to write fields; we just need to be careful to only set one in our txtpb file.

Enums

Finally, we can also write enum data. As enum types are field types, this means that, once again, we need to focus on writing fields. We already know how to do that, but there are a few points that have to be mentioned.

The first point is that we can write both an integer value and an Identifier as values. This means that if we had the following enum:

```
syntax = "proto3";

enum Type {
  MONSTER_TYPE_UNSPECIFIED = 0;
  MONSTER_TYPE_VAMPIRE = 1;
  MONSTER_TYPE_WEREWOLF = 2;
  //...
}
```

and we wanted to use the vampire value, we could set it like this:

```
type: MONSTER_TYPE_VAMPIRE
```

or like this:

```
type: 1
```

Note that the second approach is faster to write but way less explicit. It will make the reader go through the definition and check what value 1 is. It is, thus, preferable to directly write MONSTER_TYPE_ VAMPIRE.

Summary

In this chapter, we learned what Protobuf text format is and why we can use it. We saw that we could describe data as text, and Protobuf is able to read it to create a binary representation of it. This is useful for use cases where the main reader and editor of the data is a human. It lets us edit data and make sure that the data provided is valid by checking types. Finally, it lets us document the txtpb files by adding headers and comments. This helps future readers understand where they can find the proto file, the message definition for the data, and what some less descriptive parts of the data mean.

In the next chapter, we will see how to use the knowledge we have on proto files to generate code and decode binary, as well as the knowledge we have about txtpb to encode text to binary. This will be the last skill we need to be able to study the internals of serialization.

Quiz

1. For which use case is the Protobuf text format **not** the right fit?

    A. Sending data over the network.

    B. Debugging request/response payloads.

    C. Writing configuration files.

2. What does Protobuf text format help with?

    A. Making Protobuf data editable and readable by humans.

    B. Making writing data faster by removing extra characters.

    C. Writing self-documenting data.

    D. All the above.

3. What is true about maps in Protobuf?

    A. They are a completely separate concept from repeated fields.

    B. They are, in fact, just repeated fields of MapFieldEntry.

    C. They are related to oneofs.

4. Why would we prefer to use the identifier value of an enum instead of the numerical one?

    A. I would not. The numerical value is faster to write.

    B. I would, but only because we cannot use identifiers in the Protobuf Text Format.

    C. Because it is more descriptive and does not require the reader to check the proto file.

Answers

1. A
2. C
3. B
4. C

4

The Protobuf Compiler

Now that we know the Protobuf syntax and the text format, we can finally get our hands dirty and play with the Protobuf compiler. In this section, we are going to generate code from `.proto` files, get binary from Protobuf text format, and get text from Protobuf serialized data (binary files).

In this chapter, we're going to cover the following main topics:

- Downloading and installing `protoc`
- Transpiling `.proto` files
- Specifying import paths
- Encoding data to type with `--encode`
- Decoding data to type with `--decode`
- Decoding data to type, without `.proto` files, with `--decode_raw`
- What about the other flags?

By the end of this chapter, you will know how to use `protoc`'s main flags. You will know how to generate C++ (or any other supported language) code, how to tell `protoc` where to find the imported files in your `.proto` files, and how to get binary data out of data described with text format.

Technical requirements

All the code examples that you will see in this section can be found in the `Chapter4` directory in the GitHub repository (`https://github.com/PacktPublishing/Protocol-Buffers-Handbook`).

Downloading and installing protoc

> **Important note**
>
> For Windows users, I highly recommend you install `protoc` by using a package manager such as Chocolatey (`https://chocolatey.org/`) or any other one you want. Installing `protoc` header files is tricky, but they are necessary for getting Well-Known Type definitions. For Chocolatey, you should be able to run the following command:
>
> ```
> $ choco install protoc
> ```

Before even thinking about all the code generation and serialization, we need to install the compiler. Depending on your needs, there are multiple ways of doing this. I am going to show two. The first one is downloading `protoc` from the GitHub *Releases* page (`https://github.com/protocolbuffers/protobuf/releases`), and the second one is installing from a tool such as `curl` or `wget`.

GitHub Releases page

There, you will have a list of different precompiled binaries for different platforms (Linux, macOS) and for different architectures (arm, x86). For a given version, you will have a list of assets that look like this (for `protoc`):

- `protoc-$VERSION-linux-aarch_64.zip`
- `protoc-$VERSION-linux-ppcle_64.zip`
- `protoc-$VERSION-linux-s390_64.zip`
- `protoc-$VERSION-linux-x86_32.zip`
- `protoc-$VERSION-linux-x86_64.zip`
- `protoc-$VERSION-osx-aarch_64.zip`
- `protoc-$VERSION-osx-universal_binary.zip`
- `protoc-$VERSION-osx-x86_64.zip`

Once you select the asset for the version, OS, and architecture you have, you can unzip the download file. The `.zip` file content has the following structure:

```
protoc-$VERSION-$OS-$ARCH.zip
├── bin
│   └── protoc
└── include
    └── google
        └── protobuf
```

```
              ├── any.proto
              ├── api.proto
              ├── compiler
              │    └── plugin.proto
              ├── descriptor.proto
              ├── duration.proto
              ├── empty.proto
              ├── field_mask.proto
              ├── source_context.proto
              ├── struct.proto
              ├── timestamp.proto
              ├── type.proto
              └── wrappers.proto
```

If you are on Linux or macOS, you can run the following command to add the include files and binary to /usr/local:

```
$ unzip -o protoc-$VERSION-$OS-$ARCH.zip -d /usr/local bin/protoc
'include/*'
```

After that, you should be able to run the following command:

```
$ protoc --version
```

And it should print the version you just chose, like so:

```
libprotoc $VERSION
```

If you have that, your compiler is ready, and you can go to the next section.

curl and wget

Sometimes, we need to install the compiler automatically. This might be the case for DevOps or other automatization tasks. In these cases, we can use curl and wget. Now, as we know, releases of protoc are named with the following convention:

```
protoc-$VERSION-$OS-$ARCH
```

This means that we have three variables to set. We will set them temporarily at the beginning of the command like so (this example is for macOS arm64 and version 25.1):

```
PROTOC_VERSION=25.1 PROTOC_OS=osx PROTOC_ARCH=aarch_64
```

Then, we will separate the declaration of variables with a semicolon and call `curl`/`wget` with the following URL:

```
https://github.com/protocolbuffers/protobuf/releases/download/
v$PROTOC_VERSION/protoc-$PROTOC_VERSION-$PROTOC_OS-$PROTOC_ARCH.zip
```

So, in the end, we have the following command:

```
$ PROTOC_VERSION=25.1 PROTOC_OS=osx PROTOC_ARCH=aarch_64 ; wget
https://github.com/protocolbuffers/protobuf/releases/download/
v$PROTOC_VERSION/protoc-$PROTOC_VERSION-$PROTOC_OS-$PROTOC_ARCH.zip
```

After that, you can go ahead and unzip the file in your path like so (example for `/usr/local`):

```
$ unzip -o protoc-$VERSION-$OS-$ARCH.zip -d /usr/local bin/protoc
'include/*'
```

So, in the end, if you wanted to do the whole installation, you could simply run the following command:

```
$ PROTOC_VERSION=25.1 PROTOC_OS=osx PROTOC_ARCH=aarch_64 ; wget
https://github.com/protocolbuffers/protobuf/releases/download/
v$PROTOC_VERSION/protoc-$PROTOC_VERSION-$PROTOC_OS-$PROTOC_ARCH.zip &&
unzip -o protoc-$PROTOC_VERSION-$PROTOC_OS-$PROTOC_ARCH.zip -d /usr/
local bin/protoc 'include/*'
```

After that, if you want to check that the compiler is installed, you can run the following command:

```
$ protoc --version
```

And it should print the version you just chose, like so:

```
libprotoc $VERSION
```

If you have that, your compiler is ready, and you can go to the next section.

Transpiling .proto files

We are finally ready to generate some code from the `.proto` file. And even though we are going to use the compiler for other tasks, this is the main one you will use `protoc` for. In this section, we will generate code in C++ and Go. This is not a random choice. One is a directly supported language for `protoc`, and the other is supported by adding/downloading a `protoc` plugin. By seeing how to generate code for these two languages, you should be able to generate code for any other language.

Why code generation?

Before even generating code, we need to understand what the point of generating code from a .proto file is. As of now, we mostly talked about Protobuf as an abstract concept being able to serialize and deserialize data. But, in later chapters, we will start using Protobuf serialization and deserialization in code.

To do so, instead of adding a dependency and calling exposed functions, Protobuf relies on generated code to manage all calls to the lower-level library, which does the serialization/deserialization. The generated code acts as an intermediary and provides idiomatic code in the language you are using Protobuf in. It basically lets you create, access, and mutate Protobuf-generated objects in your favorite language and handles the serialization/deserialization of the data for you.

Note that I said two important things: it acts as an intermediary and it creates idiomatic code. The "acting as an intermediary" part is the most important. Without generating code, you would have to manually create structs/classes and map the binary data into the struct/class you defined. This is highly error-prone and involves a lot of work. With code generation, we do not have to do that; it manages everything for us. We just access fields from instances of object defined in the generated code.

Then, I emphasized idiomatic code because most Protobuf implementations supported by protoc are just wrappers around the C/C++ implementation. This means that if we did not have generated code, we would probably have to call some library function that looks horrible in the standard of the programming language you want to use. Now, with generated code, we do not have to deal with terseness; it feels like we are writing code in the same language all along.

Generating C++ code

Let us take the first step in using our newly installed Protobuf compiler. To generate code, we have some flags that define the output directory into which we want to generate code. We can find these flags by running the following command:

```
$ protoc --help
```

For now, we can skip most of the flags. The important ones are the following:

```
--cpp_out=OUT_DIR        Generate C++ header and source.
--csharp_out=OUT_DIR     Generate C# source file.
--java_out=OUT_DIR       Generate Java source file.
--kotlin_out=OUT_DIR     Generate Kotlin file.
--objc_out=OUT_DIR       Generate Objective-C header and source.
--php_out=OUT_DIR        Generate PHP source file.
--pyi_out=OUT_DIR        Generate python pyi stub.
--python_out=OUT_DIR     Generate Python source file.
--ruby_out=OUT_DIR       Generate Ruby source file.
--rust_out=OUT_DIR       Generate Rust sources.
```

As you can see, they have the form of ${LANG}_out. This is the convention name, and we will see that even the flags for plugins added to protoc have similar names.

So, knowing that, we can generate C++ code by running the following command:

```
$ protoc --cpp_out=. code_generation.proto
```

We will get a header and source file respectively, called code_generation.pb.h and code_generation.pb.cc.

We are going to see later how the generated code maps to the Protobuf compiler, but note that the code_generation.proto file can be found in the gen folder inside the chapter4 directory. In this file, we take advantage of Protobuf not having strict keywords. By strict keywords, I mean that a .proto file will compile if a field is named int32, which is also the name of a type. So, we can have the following field:

```
int32 int32 = 3;
```

The reason for doing this is that we will later be able to search easily in the generated code. If we want to see how int32 maps to Go code, we open the generated code and search for int32.

Do not worry too much about this right now; we will see that soon. For now, we can be happy; we generated code out of a .proto file!

Generating Go code

> **Important note**
>
> At the risk of stating the obvious, this section requires Go installed. If you do not have it yet, you can go to https://go.dev/doc/install. Note that, even if you have no intention of installing it or generating Go code, this section provides some information about protoc plugins. So, I still recommend you read it.

Generating code in a language that is not supported out of the box by protoc is very similar. However, we will need to install a protoc plugin first. These plugins are pieces of software called by protoc to generate code in a given language.

One such example of a language not supported by default is Go. Try to execute the following without the plugin:

```
$ protoc --go_out=. a.proto
```

You will get the following error:

```
protoc-gen-go: program not found or is not executable
```

So, to install it, you can run the following command:

```
$ go install google.golang.org/protobuf/cmd/protoc-gen-go@latest
```

Now, you should have a binary installed on your computer. This binary follows the `protoc-gen-${LANG}` name convention. However, running it directly will not do anything because it reads on standard input.

So, we can now run the following:

```
$ protoc --go_out=. code_generation.proto
```

We'll then get a file called `code_generation.pb.go`.

Finally, note that the plugin you install might have an independent set of options that are only relevant in the context of the chosen programming language. In Go, for example, you will have the following options:

- `paths=imports`
- `paths=relative_source`
- `module=$PREFIX`

We will not go into many details about them; you can check the documentation for them (`https://protobuf.dev/reference/go/go-generated`). However, it's important to know that some plugins expose extra configuration.

We now know how to generate code for both languages supported by default in `protoc` and ones added by plugins. This is already a good step toward using Protobuf in code.

How does the code map to the .proto file?

> **Important note**
>
> In this section, I am going to use Golang code to show the mapping between the `.proto` file and the generated Go code. If you are not familiar with Go, I generated code in the most common languages supported by Protobuf. If you do not find code for your favorite language, do not fret; remember that you have the skills to generate code by yourself.
>
> I invite you to check the generated code for your language and find the different parts that I mentioned in the section. This is a good exercise to get familiar with the generated code and not treat it as black magic.

We know how to generate code, but we do not much about generated code itself. It just feels like black magic. Let us demystify all of this and show that generated code is simpler than you might think.

Remember that we used "weird" names for our fields. We named them after the type they use. Here is a shortened version of our `code_generation.proto` file:

```
double double = 1;
float float = 2;
int32 int32 = 3;
```

This is obviously not an example of good naming. However, for learning purposes, this gives us a superpower. We can now search a little bit more easily in the generated code.

If we take the `double` example in Go-generated code, we can open `code_generation.pb.go` and search for `double`; we will find the following (simplified):

```
Double    float64   `protobuf:"fixed64,1,opt,name=double,proto3"`
```

As you can see, the generation of Go code maps a `double` type to the `float64` type. Next, you can see that it creates idiomatic code. Here, `Double` is a struct field that is exported (*D* is in capital letters). In fact, to be more precise, it is written in PascalCase; we just cannot see it for this simple example, but if you add an `another_boolean` field name, you will have the following:

```
AnotherBoolean bool //...
```

So, we transform snake_case, which is the recommended case for field names, to PascalCase, which is the way to export fields in a Go struct.

Next (I alluded to this earlier), these fields are generated in a struct. This is the way of writing types in Go. If we are looking for a message called `TestCodeGenMessage`, we will find the following:

```
type TestCodeGenMessage struct
```

It is as simple as that. Note once again that, it will generate PascalCase name out of your message name. However, since the recommended case for message names in the `.proto` file is already PascalCase, we cannot really see the difference here. Imagine we had the following message (which is against the style guide):

```
message testCodeGenMessage { /*...*/ }
```

It would still create a structure with the same name. In fact, defining both `testCodeGenMessage` and `TestCodeGenMessage` will generate twice the same struct and thus lead to a type redefinition.

Next, let us look at how enums are translated. This is even more interesting to see in Go since Go does not have an explicit enum construct like other languages. If we search for `TestCodeGenEnum`, we will get the following:

```
type TestCodeGenEnum int32

const (
```

```
TestCodeGenEnum_TEST_CODE_GEN_ENUM_UNSPECIFIED TestCodeGenEnum = 0
TestCodeGenEnum_TEST_CODE_GEN_ENUM_ANOTHER      TestCodeGenEnum = 1
)
```

As you can see, in Go, we are creating a type called `TestCodeGenEnum`, and then we have constants named `TestCodeGenEnum_${VARIANT_NAME}`. These constants will take the value of the tag defined in the `.proto` file. In our case, `TEST_CODE_GEN_ENUM_UNSPECIFIED` is defined like so:

```
enum TestCodeGenEnum {
  TEST_CODE_GEN_ENUM_UNSPECIFIED = 0;
  //...
}
```

We have a tag 0, so the constant in Go gets the value 0. This might seem insignificant right now, but it will help us understand the binary when we study the internals of serialization.

Finally, I want to mention the mapping of Well-Known Types. In our `code_generation.proto` file (in `chapter4/gen`), we use the `Duration` Well-Known Type. If we look at the field called `duration`, we have the following:

```
import (
  //...
  durationpb "google.golang.org/protobuf/types/known/durationpb"
)
//...
Duration *durationpb.Duration
```

This basically means that Protobuf Go provided generated code as part of its library. This will be the case for any other implementation. This means that we can use these Well-Known Types in our code directly too. We will do that later on in this book.

That is all about generated code. The rest of the chapter is mostly about providing helpers to work with generated types and calling the Protobuf library. We do not need to understand all of this for now. We understand that generated code is not black magic, and we should feel confident about inspecting it.

Specifying import paths

We saw that we can import files in Protobuf, but up until now, we only saw the syntax. If you do not remember, this looks like the following:

```
import "proto/a.proto";
```

Now, because the string after the `import` keyword is mostly a path, we might find ourselves with `protoc` not being aware of where this file is. This might happen in the following situations:

- We want to keep the import path "clean," meaning that we want all files in the project to be imported from a certain folder. For example, the `proto` directory is commonly used, and we could have all `.proto` files under this folder.

- If we want to build the `.proto` files in a directory that cannot directly access the `.proto` file from the current location; for example, if we wanted to have shared libraries for multiple projects.

If you used GCC or Clang in the C/C++ world, this will feel very familiar to you. If you did not, do not worry; this is as simple as it gets.

In order to import files that are in a given location, we can use the `--proto_path` flag or its short version `-I` (capital *I*). So, we could have the following `.proto` file (`a.proto`):

```
syntax = "proto3";

import "b.proto"; // this is the path

message A {
  B b = 1;
}
```

And we could have another looking like this (`b.proto`):

```
syntax = "proto3";

message B {}
```

Suppose they were next to each other in the same folder, like so:

```
.
├── a.proto
└── b.proto
```

It would compile perfectly with a simple output:

```
$ protoc --cpp_out=. a.proto
```

However, let's say that we have the following architecture:

```
.
├── a.proto
└── proto
    └── b
        └── b.proto
```

It would not compile, since from the directory in which a.proto is, we cannot access b.proto directly. If we compiled, we would get the following error:

```
b.proto: File not found.
```

In order to let protoc know where to find the file, we can use --proto_path with the proto/b value, like this:

```
$ protoc --cpp_out=. --proto_path=proto/b a.proto
```

You would think that would work, but it fails with the following error:

```
a.proto: File does not reside within any path specified using --proto_
path (or -I).  You must specify a --proto_path which encompasses this
file.  Note that the proto_path must be an exact prefix of the .proto
file names -- protoc is too dumb to figure out when two paths (e.g.
absolute and relative) are equivalent (it's harder than you think).
```

Without going into too much detail about why this is the case, protoc tells us that it basically cannot figure out if two paths are equivalent. In our case, the two paths, proto/b and the current path (.), are not equivalent, but it does not matter. protoc needs to know where all the files are. We can solve that by including the current path. We can run the following command:

```
$ protoc --cpp_out=. --proto_path=. --proto_path=proto/b a.proto
```

And, as expected, we will get our generated code.

Finally, another thing that is important to mention is that Well-Known Types should not require you to use --proto_path if you installed the protoc include files mentioned at the beginning of this chapter. Take a look at the following code:

```
syntax = "proto3";

import "google/protobuf/duration.proto";

message Test {
  google.protobuf.Duration duration = 1;
}
```

This can be simply compiled with the following:

```
$ protoc --cpp_out=. wkt.proto
```

You do not need to run the following:

```
$ protoc -I/usr/local/include …
```

You now know how to use -I and --proto_path. Everything should be clear as this is a simple flag. Let us now get fancier with the compiler.

Encoding data to type with --encode

Now, we will start to see flags that are important for learning Protobuf and inspecting the serialized data. We will start with the flag called --encode.

As its name suggests, the --encode flag is used to encode data. It will take some data and turn it into binary (serialization). This is especially useful at this point in the book because we can inspect data without having to write code yet. We simply need protoc and the knowledge we have on how to write in Protobuf Text Format.

Our goal in this section is not so much understanding the binary produced. We care about generating it first. In the next chapter, we will talk about the binary format. So, let us just write a simple textpb file and encode it with the --encode flag.

We will have the following textpb file (encode/user.txtpb):

```
id: 42
name: "Clément"
```

We will also have the following .proto file (encode/user.proto):

```
syntax = "proto3";

message User {
  uint64 id = 1;
  string name = 2;
}
```

We can now encode the .txtpb file data into a User message by executing the following command on Linux and macOS:

```
$ cat user.txtpb | protoc --encode=User user.proto
```

And we use this command on Windows:

```
$ Get-Content user.txtpb | protoc --encode=User user.proto
```

There are a few things to notice here. The first one is that the --encode flag reads on standard input. This means that we need to redirect the standard output of cat to the standard input of protoc with a pipe operator.

Next, notice that we are using the message as a value for the --encode flag. This is because we need to let protoc know which type it needs to use to encode the data. Note that if you have this type inside a package, you will need to specify the full name to the --encode flag; otherwise, it will not compile. For example, for using Well-Known Types that are under the google.protobuf package, you will need to write the following:

```
$ protoc --encode=google.proto.${TYPE_NAME} ${PATH_TO_WELL_KNOWN_TYPE}
```

And finally, we provide the .proto file in which the type is defined. In our case, we use the User type, and it happens to be defined in the user.proto file.

Now, after executing the encode command, you might not be able to see much. The main thing you should have seen is the name of the user. This is because we have the binary as the output. It turns out that only the name is printable on the screen. If you want to see the full binary in hexadecimal, you will have to use a tool. On Linux and Mac, you can run the following:

```
$ cat user.txtpb | protoc --encode=User user.proto | hexdump -C
```

And you can run the following on Windows (PowerShell):

```
$ Get-Content user.txtpb | protoc --encode=User user.proto | Format-Hex
```

This should give you an output like this:

```
08 2a 12 08 43 6c c3 a9  6d 65 6e 74
```

In the next chapter, we will look at the binary format in detail. But right now, what matters is that if you have this output, you know how to use the --encode flag.

Decoding data to type with --decode

Similarly, we have the --decode flag, which takes a binary and returns the data into text format. Once again, here, this flag is mostly for debugging and, in our case, for learning.

Now, remember that we already did the opposite of decode. This means that we will be able to take the output of encode, redirect it to decode, and we should get our input back. This would look like the following:

```
input > encode > decode > input
```

So, let us start with the encode part. We are already familiar with it; we can just execute the following command:

```
$ cat user.txtpb | protoc --encode=User user.proto
```

Or, we could execute this command:

```
$ Get-Content user.txtpb | protoc --encode=User user.proto
```

We will redirect the standard output of these commands to a file for convenience. We can do this by redirecting to a file, like so:

```
$ … > user.bin
```

With that, we can now see how to use --decode. It is very similar to --encode. It takes data on the standard input, decodes it into a type, and it needs to know where to find the type definition. It looks like this:

```
$ cat user.bin | protoc --decode=User user.proto
```

And you should get back your input (content in user.txtpb), as expected.

Finally, the same rule applies for --decode. When dealing with types that are defined in packages, you will need to provide the full name of the type. So, if you had the .txtpb file for a Duration Well-Known Type and the duration.proto file is in /usr/local/include/google/ protobuf, you would need to write something like this:

```
$ cat duration.txtpb | protoc --decode=google.protobuf.Duration /usr/
local/include/google/protobuf/duration.proto
```

You should now be ready for the next section. We will mostly work with --encode and --decode to get binary data and analyze it. In that way, we stay language agnostic, and everyone can learn without setting up a project. This minimizes the overhead and lets us focus on learning the internals.

Decoding data to type without .proto files, with --decode_ raw

The final flag that I want to present here is --decode_raw. Now, before even getting to why we would want this flag, it is important to recognize the constraints of --encode and --decode. There are two of them.

The first one is that we need to know which type the data needs to be serialized into or was serialized into. In situations where you trying to reverse engineer a solution or where you do not have much documentation, it is effectively impossible to use these two flags.

An example might be useful. Let us say that you find a file called `an_app.preferences_pb` on your Android phone (by the way, this is a real thing; check `https://developer.android.com/codelabs/android-proto-datastore`). You are not the developer of "an_app" but you still want to inspect the file and make sure that it is not storing sensitive information in "plain text." Now, you read this book, and you are thinking that you can use `--decode`. You start typing the following:

```
$ cat an_app.preferences_pb | protoc --decode=
```

And you realize that you simply cannot decode it because you do not know the encoding type.

The second constraint is that you also need to have the `.proto` file. With the same example as before, even if you knew the type into which the data was serialized, you do not have access to the `.proto` file. So, once again, you would write the following:

```
$ cat an_app.preferences_pb | protoc --decode=UserPreference
```

And you would realize that you cannot decode because you do not have that `.proto` file.

That is where `--decode_raw` comes in handy.

With the only knowledge that this file was serialized with Protobuf, we can use `--decode_raw` to get a semi-readable Protobuf Text Format output. By semi-readable, you will quickly see what I mean.

So, we just need to redirect the binary to the standard input of `protoc` and use the `--decode_raw` flag. This looks like the following:

```
$ cat an_app.preferences_pb | protoc --decode_raw
```

If you execute that, you will notice that we get something like this:

```
1: 42
2: "my very secret password"
```

Other than the fact that the developers are storing your very secret password as plain text, you can notice that the field names are gone. They are replaced by numbers. Now, knowing all you know about Protobuf, I am quite sure you guessed that these numbers are the field tags. So, as I said, this is semi-readable; we cannot be sure about what this 42 represents, but it is still handy because of the password, and we know it since, well, this is our password.

So, as you can see, even in a very constrained environment in which you do not have access to the `.proto` file and thus the type definitions, you can still inspect the data manually. This is important to keep in mind.

What about the other flags?

Obviously, after taking a look at the output of `protoc --help`, you cannot help but wonder what all these other flags are doing. For the sake of brevity, I do not cover them all here, but I thought it would be nice to mention some other flags and let you play with them. Consider this as a mini-challenge.

The first one that I particularly like is `--descriptor_set_out`. Now, we did not talk about `Descriptor` types yet. We will see them in more detail later in the book when we will manipulate them, but for now, all you need to know is that they are messages that represent Protobuf schema constructs. What this means is that we can encode the schema itself into binary.

For this mini-challenge, you will need to write a `.proto` file and encode it to binary with `--descriptor_set_out`. Once this is done, you will need to use `--decode` to inspect the content. Note that you have access to the `.proto` file where `FileDescriptorSet` (the type it serializes to) is defined; it is the `descriptor.proto` file installed along your Well-Known Types.

After the `--descriptor_set_out` flag, if you feel like going into the rabbit hole, you can take a look at `--include_imports`, `--include_source_info`, and `--retain_options`. I would not blame you if you did not, but when I was exploring all of this, it felt very good to learn about the internals.

The second flag that I want to mention is `--plugin`. For this challenge, I wrote a small `protoc` plugin that expresses how I feel about you learning that much and actually challenging yourself. However, I have been deliberately bad. I did not follow the convention of naming the plugin `protoc-gen-${LANGUAGE}`. I named it `challenge`. You will need to find a way to map the binary challenge to `protoc-gen-challenge` (without renaming the binary file!). On top of this, the challenge binary is not in your `PATH` environment, so `protoc` does not know where to find it.

Note that I have the source code of the plugin in open source. I do not expect you to trust me blindly. If you do, you can run the provided binary (in `chapter4/challenge`), or you can also build the binary from source. To do that, you will need to have Go installed, step into the `challenge` folder, and run the following:

```
$ go build .
```

You should now have the challenge binary.

Finally, you might find yourself in a situation where you have the following error message:

```
Missing output directives.
```

If this is the case, you are very close to getting the answer. However, you still need to think about what the plugins are used for and how to use them to do the task they are supposed to execute. If you need a hint, take a look at the *Generating Go code* section of this chapter, where we installed the `protoc-gen-go` plugin. Once installed, what were we able to do that we could not do before?

So, for this mini-challenge, you will need to find out what I think about you by executing this plugin. Have fun!

Summary

In this chapter, we learned how to use `protoc` to generate code and serialize/deserialize data. We saw that we can generate code for directly supported languages and ones that need plugins installed. We then saw how to encode and decode data when we have access to the `.proto` file and, therefore, the type definitions. And finally, we saw that even if we do not have the `.proto` file and type definitions, we can get a semi-readable text format output, to help us get a feel about what data is encoded.

In the next chapter, we will learn the serialization internals. We will dive deep into the binary and understand how each kind of data is serialized/deserialized. This will use the skills that we learned in this chapter to get that new knowledge.

Quiz

1. What is the short version of the `--proto_path` flag?

   A. `-I`

   B. `-p`

   C. `-1`

2. Which flag would generate Java code?

   A. `--java-out`

   B. `--java-gen-out`

   C. `--java_out`

3. When would you use `--decode_raw` instead of `--decode`?

   A. When I do not have access to the `.proto` file

   B. When I do not know into which type the data was serialized into

   C. Both of these

Answers

1. A

2. C

3. C

Challenge solutions

Challenge 1 – Descriptors

In this challenge, we need to use the `--descriptor_set_out` flag to generate binary out of our schema. Let us define a simple schema (`name.proto`):

```
syntax = "proto3";

message Name {
    string name = 1;
}
```

To generate a `FileDescriptorSet` out of it, we need to run the following command:

```
$ protoc --descriptor_set_out=name.desc name.proto
```

This will create a `name.desc` file that we can then analyze.

Now, the second step is to use `--decode` to set the internals of the `FileDescriptorSet`. To do that, assuming that you have the `descriptor.proto` file in `/usr/local/include/google/protobuf`, you can run the following:

```
$ cat name.desc | protoc -I/usr/local/include/google/protobuf
--decode=google.protobuf.FileDescriptorSet /usr/local/include/google/
protobuf/descriptor.proto
```

This should output something like this:

```
file {
  name: "name.proto"
  message_type {
    name: "Name"
    field {
      name: "name"
      number: 1
      label: LABEL_OPTIONAL
      type: TYPE_STRING
      json_name: "name"
    }
  }
  syntax: "proto3"
}
```

All of this is amazing; we serialized Protobuf language to binary!

--retain_options

The next thing we can do is use the --retain_options flag. Now, obviously, we did not use any option in the name.proto file, so it would not output anything. Let us add the deprecated option to the name field, just like so:

```
syntax = "proto3";

message Name {
    string name = 1 [deprecated = true];
}
```

We will then create a descriptor out of the .proto file by running the following:

```
$ protoc --descriptor_set_out=name_with_options.desc --retain_options
name.proto
```

And we rerun this decode command:

```
$ cat name_with_options.desc | protoc -I/usr/local/include/google/
protobuf --decode=google.protobuf.FileDescriptorSet /usr/local/
include/google/protobuf/descriptor.proto
```

We should then get the following:

```
file {
  name: "name.proto"
  message_type {
    name: "Name"
    field {
      name: "name"
      number: 1
      label: LABEL_OPTIONAL
      type: TYPE_STRING
      options {
        deprecated: true
      }
      json_name: "name"
    }
  }
  syntax: "proto3"
}
```

We now also have our options serialized into binary.

--include_imports

Similarly, we can serialize our imports. Let us first add an import to the name.proto file. We now have the following:

```
syntax = "proto3";

import "google/protobuf/empty.proto";

message Name {
  string name = 1 [deprecated = true];
  google.protobuf.Empty empty = 2; // use the import
}
```

We can then create our descriptor file:

```
$ protoc --descriptor_set_out=name_with_imports.desc --include_imports
name.proto
```

We then run the following:

```
$ cat name_with_imports.desc | protoc -I/usr/local/include/google/
protobuf --decode=google.protobuf.FileDescriptorSet /usr/local/
include/google/protobuf/descriptor.proto
```

We will get the following text format:

```
file {
  name: "google/protobuf/empty.proto"
  package: "google.protobuf"
  message_type {
    name: "Empty"
  }
  #...
  syntax: "proto3"
}
file {
  name: "name.proto"
  dependency: "google/protobuf/empty.proto"
  message_type {
    #...
  }
  syntax: "proto3"
}
```

We now have a self-contained descriptor file.

--include_source_info

Finally, we can also get more information about the layout of the .proto file. This is called SourceCodeInfo. We do not need to modify the name.proto file in this case; we can just create our descriptor:

```
$ protoc --descriptor_set_out=name_with_sci.desc --include_source_info
name.proto
```

We run the following:

```
$ cat name_with_sci.desc | protoc -I/usr/local/include/google/protobuf
--decode=google.protobuf.FileDescriptorSet /usr/local/include/google/
protobuf/descriptor.proto
```

We get the following output:

```
file {
  name: "name.proto"
  dependency: "google/protobuf/empty.proto"
  message_type {
  #...
  }
  source_code_info {
    location {
      span: 0
      span: 0
      span: 7
      span: 1
    }
    location {
      path: 12
      span: 0
      span: 0
      span: 18
    }
    #...
  }
  syntax: "proto3"
}
```

Now, the output of this command is pretty big and frightening. However, this is very interesting to understand, so I will explain the first and second locations in the `source_code_info` message.

The first location represents the whole file. In this case, we can see that we have spans. These spans can come by 3 or 4. They represent respectively the start line, start column, end line, and end column. If the end line is omitted, Protobuf will assume that the end line is the same as the start line. So, for the first location, we have the start line and start column at 0, the end line at 7, and the end column at 1. If you look at your file, you will see that this is the beginning and end of your file. Note that all the spans start at 0.

The second location represents the `syntax` statement. I will let you check the spans, but what's important here is the path. A path is a succession of numbers that are the tags of fields starting from `FileDescriptorProto`. If we look at `FileDescriptorProto` (in `descriptor.proto`), we can see the following:

```
message FileDescriptorProto {
  //...
  optional string syntax = 12;
  //...
}
```

So, we know it is a `syntax` statement.

If you are that far into the challenge, you are interested in this kind of thing. Thus, I recommend you start looking at the other locations and try to figure out how all the paths are made. Also, reading the documentation in `descriptor.proto` is very helpful!

Challenge 2 – Plugins

Finally, we come to *Challenge 2*. In this challenge, we need to use the plugin called `challenge`. It is not named appropriately. It should be called `protoc-gen-challenge`, and it is not in our PATH environment, so `protoc` cannot find it. To solve that problem, we think that we can execute the following command:

```
$ protoc --plugin=protoc-gen-challenge=./challenge challenge.proto
```

Unfortunately, we get the following error:

```
Missing output directives.
```

This is because it is not enough to specify where to find the plugin; we also need to use it. The plugin now named `protoc-gen-challenge`, at least from what `protoc` knows, provides us with the `--challenge_out` flag. So, we run the following command:

```
$ protoc --plugin=protoc-gen-challenge=./challenge --challenge_out=.
Challenge.proto
```

And we get this nice message:

```
You are awesome! It's only chapter 4 and you already have all these
skills!
```

5

Serialization Internals

Now that we know how to describe data in Protobuf text format and encode it into binary, we have all the tools we need to learn about the serialization internals. These internals are important to learn because there are a lot of trade-offs between the different types and we need to be aware of them to define efficient schemas.

In this chapter, we're going to cover the following main topics:

- Variable-length integers
- ZigZag encoding
- Fixed-size integers
- How to choose between integer types
- Length-delimited encoding
- Packed versus unpacked repeated fields
- Maps

By the end of this chapter, you will know how Protobuf encodes/decodes data to/from binary and you will understand the output binary by yourself.

Technical requirements

All the code examples that you will see in this chapter can be found in the `chapter5` directory in this book's GitHub repository (`https://github.com/PacktPublishing/Protocol-Buffers-Handbook`).

Variable-length integers (varints)

As you are now aware, the payloads that are created by Protobuf are significantly smaller than the other popular data formats. One of the biggest factors of such small payloads is the use of **variable-length integers** (**varints**). Now, let's not get ahead of ourselves. Before explaining how all of this works in Protobuf itself, let's understand the idea of varints; then, we will see where they're used in Protobuf.

As its name suggests, a varint is the concept of encoding integers into different byte sizes. What is not clear from the name is how it decides the length of the encoding. So, we are going to use an example to understand how that works.

First, we can see the result of encoding by using the skills we learned in previous chapters. We can write the following proto file (`varint/encoding.proto`):

```
syntax = "proto3";

message Encoding {
    int32 i32 = 1;
}
```

Then, we can define the data in a `txtpb` file (`varint/int32.txtpb`), like so:

```
i32: 128
```

Now that we have that, we can run `protoc` with the `--encode` flag and see the result. On Linux/Mac, we can run the following command:

```
$ cat int32.txtpb | protoc --encode=Encoding encoding.proto | hexdump
-C
```

> **Important message**
>
> Unfortunately, PowerShell does not deal well with external commands like protoc. As such, I will not provide Windows commands by fear of misleading PowerShell users. At the time of writing this, the best way to follow the following sections on Windows is to use Windows Subsystem for Linux (WSL).

We should get `08 80 01` as our hexadecimal. For now, I will ask you to trust me and only focus on `80 01`. The rest is metadata, and we will talk about it later in this chapter.

So, now that we know we need to get `80  01`, we can see how to encode 128 into varint by hand. The number 128 is deliberately chosen and not random; you will see why in a bit. We will start by displaying the number in binary:

```
10000000
```

Then, as Protobuf is encoding the actual number in the lower 7 bits of each byte, we will split the binary into groups of 7 bits. This gives us the following output:

```
0000001 0000000
```

Now, Protobuf encodes data in little-endian (the least significant byte at the smallest address). However, we are currently in big-endian (the least significant byte at the largest address). So, we will reverse all the bytes. We now have the following:

```
0000000 0000001
```

Finally, Protobuf uses the **most significant bit** (**MSB**) to know if there is another byte after the current byte. If the MSB is 1, there is; otherwise, it is the last byte. In our case, we have 2 bytes. So, there will be a 1 as the MSB of the first byte and an MSB set to 0 for the second byte. We now get the following:

```
10000000 00000001
```

That's all there is to it – we encoded 128 in varint. In hexadecimal, this would be `0x80  0x01`.

Now, let's do the opposite and decode 128. We know that encoded, 128 looks like this:

```
10000000 00000001
```

The first step is to drop the MSBs because they are only here to tell us how many bytes we have:

```
0000000 0000001
```

Now, we can turn the whole thing into big-endian by reversing all the bytes:

```
0000001 0000000
```

By doing this, we get our 128 back.

To summarize, we have the following for encoding:

```
         10000000 // Original input (big-endian).
  0000001  0000000 // Split into 7-bits groups
  0000000  0000001 // Convert to little-endian
10000000 00000001 // Add MSBs
```

We have the following for decoding:

```
10000000 00000001 // Original input (little-endian)
 0000000  0000001 // Drop MSBs.
 0000001  0000000 // Convert to big-endian
   00000010000000 // Concatenate
              128 // Result
```

So, as we saw, 128 is encoded into 2 bytes. This is because we are using the base 128 varints. This means that we have the following mappings between values and size in bytes:

Threshold Values	Size (in Bytes)
0	0
1	1
128	2
16,384	3
2,097,152	4
268,435,456	5
34,359,738,368	6
4,398,046,511,104	7
562,949,953,421,312	8
72,057,594,037,927,936	9

Now that you've seen the table in the context of this example, you might not be impressed by the result, and that's understandable. An unsigned 8-bit integer (uint8, u8, and so on) is doing even better. It can encode the value 256 into only 1 byte. However, this is important and that is why we now have to go back to see how this fits into Protobuf.

Here's the list of types that use varint as their encoding:

- int32/int64
- uint32/uint64
- sint32/sint64 (more on that in the next section)
- bool
- enum values

The majority of types are traditionally encoded in fixed size. 32-bit integers are encoded into 4 bytes (because 4 bytes is 4*8 or 32 bits) and 64-bit integers are encoded into 8 bytes. However, in Protobuf, the 32 and 64 prefixes do not define the encoding length in terms of bits – it tells us the range of numbers that we can store in these types. The ranges are what you are used to with classical 32- and 64-bit integers. However, because I am pretty sure that you do not have these numbers in mind, here are the ranges per type:

Type	Min	Max
uint32	0	4,294,967,295
uint64	0	18,446,744,073,709,551,615
int32	-2,147,483,648	2,147,483,647
int64	-9,223,372,036,854,775,808	9,223,372,036,854,775,807
sint32	-2,147,483,648	2,147,483,647
sint64	-9,223,372,036,854,775,808	9,223,372,036,854,775,807

Now that we know this, I want you to focus on these two lines (from the previous table) and think about what could be the problem of encoding in varint:

268,435,456	5
72,057,594,037,927,936	9

I am sure that you got it. Even though we have the possibility of encoding numbers into fewer bytes than fixed-size encoding, we also have the possibility of encoding them into more bytes. A number such as 268,435,456, in a classic 32-bit number, would be encoded into 4 bytes; here, it is encoded in 5. Similarly, 72,057,594,037,927,936 could be encoded into 8 with a 64-bit integer but it is encoded in 9. Later in this chapter, we will touch on how to properly choose the integer type for your data, but for now, it is just important to understand the trade-off that varint encoding has.

Another trade-off is that negative numbers encoded as binary 2's complement (it uses the binary digit with the greatest place value as the sign to indicate whether the binary number is positive or negative) are represented as large numbers and thus encoded in a lot of bytes. This is the case for int32 and int64.

Let's see the example for -1. First of all, remember that if an MSB is set to 1, this means that we have a byte following. This means that with the following binary 2s complement for –1 ():

```
11111111 11111111 11111111 11111111
```

We need to add one more byte after because we have a 1 as our MSB. Now, remember that we are in 2's complement, so we will add 11111111. We now have the following:

```
11111111 11111111 11111111 11111111 11111111
```

Once again, we need to add another byte because the MSB is 1. You can see that it could go indefinitely. Fortunately, the maximum number of bytes into which a number could be encoded is 9. And remember, that we need to finish with a byte that has an MSB set to 0 to tell that there are no bytes after.

This means that -1, even though it is a small number, will be encoded into 10 bytes:

```
11111111 11111111 11111111 11111111 11111111
11111111 11111111 11111111 11111111 00000001
```

Don't sweat it here. This doesn't mean that you cannot use negative numbers in Protobuf. There is a solution to this problem, and this solution is called ZigZag encoding.

ZigZag encoding

As we saw in the previous section, int32 and int64 are not efficient at storing negative numbers. They will always result in 10-byte-long payloads. To solve this specific use case of negative numbers, Protobuf introduces two other types: sint32 and sint64. The "s" stands for signed and they handle negative numbers.

The reason why they handle negative numbers more efficiently is that they add an extra step on top of varint encoding. This extra step, called ZigZag encoding, consists of turning all negative numbers into positive ones, and because varint encoding is very good at encoding positive numbers, we solved the problem.

Now, as usual, let's see an example of ZigZag encoding. Let's take our cherished 128. We have the following binary:

```
00000000 10000000
```

Now, let's left shift by one:

```
00000001 00000000
```

We will then take the original binary and apply a right shift of 31 in the case of int32 and 63 in the case of int64. In our case, we will get the following output:

```
00000000 00000000
```

Finally, we will apply an exclusive or (XOR) on the two shifts results. We'll get the following output:

```
00000001 00000000
```

So, 128 will be transformed into 256. Following all these steps, the varint encoding will encode this number into 2 bytes (see the table in the previous section).

Now, let's decode the result we got previously. We currently have the following:

```
00000001 00000000
```

Let's do a right shift by one:

```
00000000 10000000
```

Next, we'll take the original binary and apply an AND with a value of 1:

```
00000000 00000000
```

We take the absolute value of the previous binary (-0 or 0) and do an XOR between it and the first shift:

```
00000000 10000000
```

We now have our 128 back.

To summarize, we have the following for encoding:

```
00000000 10000000 // I = Original input.
00000001 00000000 // A = I << 1
00000000 00000000 // B = I >> 31
00000001 00000000 // A ^ B
              256 // Result
```

We have the following for decoding:

```
00000001 00000000 // I = Original input
00000000 10000000 // A = I >> 1
00000000 00000000 // B = -(I & 1)
00000000 10000000 // A ^ B
              128 // Result
```

Now, to understand a little bit more about the trade-offs that this is creating, let's take a look at a table showing the encoding of the range -5 to 5:

Original	Encoded
-5	9
-4	7
-3	5
-2	3
-1	1
0	0
1	2
2	4
3	6
4	8
5	10

As we can see, we are interleaving positive and negative number encodings. All the negative numbers will get an odd value, and the positive values will get an even one.

Now that we know that property, and we know that ZigZag encoding is acting as an intermediary step before varint, we can think about what it means for our final encoding. Essentially, you can think of ZigZag encoding as turning a range from MIN_INT32 to MAX_INT32 into a range of 0 to MAX_UINT32 under the hood. However, the range that you can access as a user of this type is still MIN_INT32 to MAX_INT32. Thus, ZigZag encoding is considered less effective in encoding positive numbers than varint alone; given the same underlying range (0 to MAX_UINT32), varint can encode twice as many positive values. In ZigZag encoding, half of the range is taken by negative numbers turned into positives.

I am sure that the trade-off we have here is a little bit confusing to understand at first. Don't worry too much about this – we are going to cover some rules to follow on how to choose the right integer type. However, I would still encourage you to think about the difference between the range of numbers that we can use as users of the sint32 type (MIN_INT32 to MAX_INT32) and the underlying representation of its value (uint32). You should conclude that, with the same underlying representation (uint32), you would maximize the number of positive numbers that you can encode with varint.

Fixed-size integers

The last type of integer type we'll look at is the fixed-size integer type. These are pretty much encoded how integers/floating points are encoded into your computer memory. In this case, the 32 and 64 suffixes of the type names correspond to the number of bits the value will be encoded in.

The types that are encoded into fixed-size integers are fixed32, fixed64, sfixed32, sfixed64, float, and double. The main thing to talk about here is the difference between sfixed and fixed. The former is signed, meaning that it can contain positive and negative numbers. The latter is unsigned, which means it can only contain positive numbers.

Let's look at an example, just to ensure that we're on the same page about encoding fixed-size numbers. If we have the following message (`fixed/encoding.proto`):

```
syntax = "proto3";

message Encoding {
    fixed32 f32 = 1;
}
```

We set the value 128 to `f32` (`fixed32.txtpb`):

```
f32: 128
```

We run the encoding like so:

```
$ cat fixed32.txtpb | protoc --encode=Encoding encoding.proto |
hexdump -C
0d 80 00 00 00
```

We get `80 00 00 00` (forget about the leading `0d` for now). If you check the decimal representation of `80`, you will see that it is equal to 128. Not surprising.

Now, we know that varint has potential overhead when encoding large numbers. For example, the numbers above and including 268,435,456 will be encoded as 5 bytes in varint and only in 4 using fixed32. Similarly, numbers above and including 72,057,594,037,927,936 will be encoded as 9 bytes in varint but only 8 with fixed64. This is another trade-off that we need to be aware of when choosing integer types.

How to choose between integer types

Now that we know the two major algorithms behind integer encoding, we can reflect a little bit on how to choose between them. We will cover the three considerations that we need to think about when we decide between the integer types: number range, sign, and data distribution.

Number range

As we saw, Protobuf's 32 and 64 suffixes on integer type names do not always represent the number of bits it takes to encode a value. We saw that it is better to think about them as the range of values that can be encoded.

This means that, when choosing an integer type, we need to be aware of the range of values needed for a specific use case. Let's consider three examples:

- Number of employees in a company
- Request per second metric
- Non-reusable IDs

For the first one, we can assume that our company will have less than 2 billion employees. The biggest companies in terms of employees, at the time of writing this book, have ~2 million employees. Furthermore, having 2 billion employees would mean that you employ a fourth of the world's population. This is, at least for me, unimaginable. Now, having set these assumptions, we can safely choose an int32 (there is a better choice; more about that later). We know that we will never need the full range to encode the number of employees in a company.

For the second example, let's step into the shoes of an engineer at Google dealing with global-scale APIs. If we wanted to encode the metric "request per second," we would need to deal with values that are in the tens of billions (see `https://cloud.google.com/blog/products/gcp/grpc-a-true-internet-scale-rpc-framework-is-now-1-and-ready-for-production-deployments`). As such, we would not be able to use an int32 or uint32 for such a metric – we would need to switch to an int64 (or uint64) to be safe.

Finally, let's think about some IDs that are not directly reusable. For example, we could think about bank transactions. Because we can't reuse IDs (at least not for an extended period), we might well end up with more than MAX_INT64 or even MAX_UINT64. In that case, the answer to "What integer type should I choose?" is you choose neither of them. Google recommends using strings for these kinds of IDs and this makes sense for these kinds of use cases.

As you can see, you will need to be aware of the data you have and make some assumptions about the data you will receive. Once you do your homework, it will be trivial to choose between 32- and 64-bit integer types.

Sign

In Protobuf, another way of selecting the range of values we can handle is by selecting the sign of an integer type. For those of you who are familiar with most statically typed languages, you are already familiar with this. We can choose between an unsigned int (uint) and an int.

For this case, let's consider some examples:

- User's age
- Temperature

For the first one, we all know that an age cannot be negative. Thus, we will be choosing an unsigned int. That is trivial but very important. If we chose an integer and a client was mistakenly sending a negative number, we would be getting a 10-byte encoding whereas we would get 1 byte otherwise (we can safely assume that age is less than 128). On top of the property of being protected against such large payloads due to mistakes, by using a uint, we can, in compiled languages, provide feedback at compile time for developers to avoid these mistakes. If they were trying to pass a negative value to an uint, in a lot of cases, the code wouldn't even compile.

For the second example, we know that the temperature can be negative or positive. As such, we will choose an integer and not an unsigned integer. Of course, we need to combine this with the work we did on number ranges to decide whether we want an int32 or an int64. If we are talking about the temperature on Earth, we can safely assume that we can use an int32.

Once again, we need to understand our data. If we have negative numbers, we choose a signed integer; otherwise, we choose an unsigned one. And with this choice being combined with the previous one on number ranges, it will give you an integer type (int32, uint32, int64, or uint64). The last thing we need to talk about is how to choose between sints and fixed integer types.

Data distribution

So far, we've talked about criteria that are easy to understand if you come from statically typed languages. In this setup, we're making these choices almost every day. However, this last criterion is not something that we are used to because it comes from the trade-offs created by the encoding algorithms that we saw earlier (varint and ZigZag).

As data distribution is very specific to use cases, I will be using a use case that I worked on. This will show the kind of improvement that we can have. After that, I will list some considerations that we need to be aware of when choosing between sints and fixed integer types.

Let's start with the example. After reading a blog post comparing JSON and Protobuf for a Wi-Fi site survey, I noticed a potential improvement that I could implement to help the company. Let's look at the proto file:

```
syntax = "proto3";

message WiFiSiteSurvey {
  uint32 timestamp = 1;
  repeated AP accesspoints = 2;
}

message AP {
  int64 mac = 1;
  string ssid = 2;
  int32 rssi = 3;
```

```
    int32 channel = 4;
}
```

The improvement that I thought about was related to unpacked versus packed repeated fields (more on that later). In this case, I was thinking about optimizing the accesspoints fields.

While it turned out to be an impractical improvement, I started to dig into the data and noticed that the rssi field could only contain negative values between -30 and -90. With the knowledge that we have now on how negative numbers are encoded with the int32 type, we know that this is a bad idea. Each time we set a value to the field, it will be encoded as 10 bytes. We know that we should use a sint32 here.

Before the improvement, the comparison with the JSON payload was as follows:

```
Found Aps 30
JSON payload length: 1949 bytes
Protobuf payload length: 966 bytes
```

It is already quite efficient. We have ~2 times fewer bytes with Protobuf.

But after adding a "s" before the int32 type for rssi, we got the following:

```
Found APs 30
JSON payload length: 1949 bytes
Protobuf payload length: 713 bytes
```

Another ~200 bytes were shaved off.

This clearly shows that choosing your integer types properly is important and this can only be done by understanding the underlying encoding algorithms and the data distribution.

Now, there are more things to consider. Here's a list:

- The ratio of positive/negative numbers. We might be ok with suffering a 10-byte encoding of a negative value from time to time. If the majority of values are positive numbers and the number of negative numbers is not above a certain threshold, we could use an int32. Otherwise, we can start using a sint32.

- The ratio of small/big numbers. As we saw, varint will encode the smallest values into a smaller number of bytes. However, it can also encode bigger values into more bytes than a fixed-sized int. We need to be aware of that and if the majority of numbers we are dealing with are encoded in more than 4 or 8 bytes, we could use a fixed32 or a fixed64. Otherwise, we can still use varints.

As you can see, choosing an integer type is not easy. However, after taking into consideration, the range, the sign, and the data distribution, we can make an educated choice. While some choices are very familiar to people who work with statically typed languages, others are harder to make because they require a lot of knowledge of the data. The most important thing to keep in mind is to know your data and take the time to design your schemas properly. It can save you a lot of bandwidth and thus a lot of money.

Field metadata

So far, we haven't talked too much about field tags. In this section, we'll dive into how they are encoded and why they are encoded as such.

First, let's get a small refresher on what field tags are. They are identifiers for fields that will help Protobuf know into which field to deserialize some data. So, let's say we have the following field:

```
uint64 id = 1;
```

Protobuf decodes some specific data with an ID of 1 (tag), so it will know that this data is meant to be deserialized into the id field. All of this is an abstract explanation of what's happening, so let's understand concretely how the field for deserialization is selected.

First, we need to understand that Protobuf only serializes a combination of type, tag, and value. The name of a field is not serialized. We already know how integer values get serialized; later, we will see how it works for other types (string, repeated, and so on). For now, we can focus on how the type and tag are encoded.

So, let's see an example. Let's say that we have a simple `int32` field (`metadata/encoding.proto`):

```
syntax = "proto3";

message Encoding {
  int32 i32 = 1;
}
```

Let's describe the data that we want in the `i32` field (`metadata/varint.txtpb`):

```
i32: 128
```

Now, we can get the hexadecimal representation of the binary:

```
$ cat varint.txtpb | protoc --encode=Encoding encoding.proto | hexdump
-C
08 80 01
```

As we know, int32 is encoded as varint and thus 128 is encoded as 2 bytes (80 01). So, what is this 08 prefix? It is a bitpacking of the field type and the field tag. This means that, in this case, we store this 2 information in a single byte. We store the type in the first 3 bits of the byte and the rest represents the tag encoded as a varint.

Let's take a look at the binary for 08:

```
0000 1000
```

This means that the type is the following part of the binary:

```
0000 1000
```

And consequently, the rest is the tag. This means that we have the tag being equal to 1 and the type is equal to 0.

Here's a list of mapping between types and their number representations:

ID	Name	Used For
0	VARINT	int32, int64, uint32, uint64, sint32, sint64, bool, enum
1	I64	fixed64, sfixed64, double
2	LEN	string, bytes, embedded messages, packed repeated fields
3	SGROUP	group start (deprecated)
4	EGROUP	group end (deprecated)
5	I32	fixed32, sfixed32, float

In our example, we knew that int32 was encoded as varint and it is confirmed here because we have an ID of 0, which maps to VARINT.

Now, you might have noticed that I said, "In this case, we store these 2 information into a single byte." I emphasize the "in this case" part because, as mentioned previously, the tag itself is encoded as varint. This means that the metadata of a field could take more than one byte if the tag gets big enough. Here's a table for the thresholds at which the metadata payload grows:

Tag	Size (in bytes)
1	1
16	2
2,048	3
262144	4
33554432	5
536870911 (max)	5

We can see that before encoding the metadata into 2 bytes, we have 15 tags that have a low overhead, but after passing a tag of 16, we start to get more and more overhead.

Generally, we try to keep the number of tags as low as possible to lower the overhead. If you take a look at the proto files provided by Google as part of protoc, you will see that most of the messages are using under 16 tags. This is mostly done by splitting big messages into multiple messages. And, as with everything, it introduces some trade-offs that we are going to discuss in the next section.

Length-delimited encoding

So far, we've seen how to encode values that have static sizes. For example, when dealing with the encoding of an int32, Protobuf deals with 4 bytes and turns them into a variable number of bytes. The same is true with other number types. In this section, we are going to learn how to encode a value that has a dynamic size. In other words, a size that can only be determined at runtime.

The types with such a dynamic size are strings and bytes. However, some other parts of Protobuf are encoded with length-delimited encoding: embedded messages and packed repeated fields. We are going to talk about the latter in the next section, but we are going to see strings and embedded messages here.

Let's look at an example of encoding strings in Protobuf. Once again, we are going to create a message (`length_delimited/encoding.proto`):

```
syntax = "proto3";

message Encoding {
  string s = 1;
}
```

We're also going to describe the data in text format (`length_delimited/string.txtpb`):

```
s: "Hello World!"
```

Finally, we can get the hexadecimal representation of the binary:

```
$ cat string.txtpb | protoc --encode=Encoding encoding.proto | hexdump
-C
0a 0c 48 65 6c 6c 6f 20  57 6f 72 6c 64 21
```

If you are familiar with ASCII, you've probably noticed that we have the string value as ASCII:

48	65	6c	6c	6f	20	57	6f	72	6c	64	21
H	e	l	l	o	<space>	W	o	r	l	d	!

This leaves us with 0a 0c at the front of the payload. From experience, we know that one of them must be the field metadata (type and tag). This is the first byte. We have the following:

```
OA = 0000 1010
```

This means we have a type of 2 (LEN for length-delimited) and a tag of 1. There are no surprises there – we learned all of that.

The second byte, as you might have guessed, is the length of the string (OC = 12). This is as simple as that. To conclude, we have the following encoding pattern:

```
<tag+type> <length> <value>
```

Now, as I mentioned, embedded messages are also encoded in length-delimited format. First, let's see what an embedded message is (length_delimited/encoding.proto):

```
syntax = "proto3";

message Encoding {
    string s = 1;
    Embedded e = 2;

    message Embedded {
        int32 i32 = 1;
    }
}
```

Here, Embedded is a nested message and the e field is an embedded message. It embeds a message value in another message.

Now, let's try to encode the following data into the e field (length_delimited/embedded.txtpb):

```
e: {
    i32: 128
}
```

We can run the following command to get the hexadecimal representation of the binary:

```
$ cat embedded.txtpb | protoc --encode=Encoding encoding.proto |
hexdump -C
12 03 08 80 01
```

Recall that the i field is encoded as 08 80 01, where 08 is the tag+type combination and 80 01 is the varint encoding of 128. We also know that the 03 value preceding that is the length in bytes of the value.

Finally, we have 12, which can be represented in binary as follows:

```
0001 0010
```

We have the LEN type and a tag of 2.

Now that we know how to encode dynamic size items in Protobuf, it is important to understand a few things. The first thing to understand is that the length is encoded as varint. This means that, for example, if you had a string that is 128 characters long, the size would take 2 bytes.

The second important consideration is related to what we mentioned here and in the previous section. We talked about the fact that field tags are encoded as varints. This means that having messages with a lot of fields could result in overheads. I mentioned that we could split messages to get fewer tags per message. However, we also saw that embedded messages have extra byte(s) encoded just after the tag+type byte(s). This means that splitting and embedding messages is not necessarily advantageous in terms of byte size, you will have to keep that in mind and see if it makes sense for your use case.

Packed versus unpacked repeated fields

One last important concept that is important to know is the concept of packed and unpacked repeated fields. As we know, repeated is the way we describe lists in Protobuf. A repeated modifier can be applied to a scalar type (int32, uint64, and so on) but can also be applied to more complex types (user-defined types, strings, and so on). The former will be encoded as a packed repeated field, and the latter will be unpacked.

Before going into more detail, let's visualize the difference between both encodings. Let's start with a packed repeated field. We will have a list of integers (repeated/encoding.proto):

```
syntax = "proto3";

message Encoding {
   repeated uint64 us = 1;
}
```

We can now set some values for it by describing the data in text format (repeated/packed.txtpb):

```
us: [1, 2, 3, 4, 5]
```

Now, let's run the following command:

```
$ cat packed.txtpb | protoc --encode=Encoding encoding.proto | hexdump
-C
0a 05 01 02 03 04 05
```

As we can see, we have the list encoded as length-delimited. We have a length of 05 followed by the values and 0a representing the LEN type with a tag of 1. This is a packed repeated field because we are packing all the values together under the same tag+type.

Now, let's see what happens when we consider a repeated field of a more complex type. For example, we can do a list of strings (repeated/encoding.proto):

```
syntax = "proto3";

message Encoding {
    repeated string ss = 2;
}
```

Then, we can describe the data in text format (repeated/unpacked.txtpb):

```
ss: ["1", "2", "3", "4", "5"]
```

Now, let's run the following command:

```
$ cat unpacked.txtpb | protoc --encode=Encoding encoding.proto |
hexdump -C
12 01 31 12 01 32 12 01  33 12 01 34 12 01 35
```

You might be able to see a pattern in the hexadecimal. We seem to always be repeating the 12 01 sequence. This is an unpacked repeated field. Because, in this case, strings have a dynamic size, we cannot determine the length of the whole repeated field, so we encode each item in the list as length-delimited elements (as a string should). This causes this overhead of always repeating the same bytes (here, 12 01), whereas, in the packed repeated field, we could have that metadata mentioned only once.

Now, this doesn't mean you should never use a repeated field on complex types. But you should be aware of the intrinsic overhead that it causes. If you can avoid it, just avoid it; otherwise, simply accept the cost.

Maps

Finally, we can talk about how maps are encoded in Protobuf. In *Chapter 3* on Protobuf text format, I briefly mentioned that a map is a list of objects that contains the key and value fields. In this section, we are going to dive deeper into this and see how maps are encoded.

First, let's not take for granted that a map is a list of objects. Let's investigate that. We can define a message containing a map field (map/encoding.proto):

```
syntax = "proto3";

message Encoding {
```

```
    map<string, int32> m = 1;
}
```

Now, to see how this translates internally, we can turn that proto file into a descriptor file. Protoc has a flag called `--descriptor_set_out` for doing that. Let's create a descriptor file called `encoding.desc`:

```
$ protoc --descriptor_set_out=encoding.desc encoding.proto
```

This file contains a binary of `FileDescriptorSet`, which is a message defined in the `descriptor.proto` file provided with protoc. Now, we can decode this descriptor file with the following command:

> **Important message**
>
> If you followed *Chapter 4* and installed protoc like it was described there, you can replace the following `${PATH_TO_PROTO_INCLUDES}` with `/usr/local/include/google/protobuf`. Otherwise, you will have to remember where you stored the include folder and append `google/protobuf` to its path.

```
$ cat encoding.desc | protoc --decode=google.protobuf.
FileDescriptorSet -I${PATH_TO_PROTO_INCLUDES} ${PATH_TO_PROTO_
INCLUDES}/descriptor.proto
file {
  name: "encoding.proto"
  message_type {
    name: "Encoding"
    field {
      name: "m"
      number: 1
      label: LABEL_REPEATED
      type: TYPE_MESSAGE
      type_name: ".Encoding.MEntry"
      json_name: "m"
    }
    nested_type {
      name: "MEntry"
      field {
        name: "key"
        number: 1
        label: LABEL_OPTIONAL
        type: TYPE_STRING
        json_name: "key"
      }
      field {
```

```
      name: "value"
      number: 2
      label: LABEL_OPTIONAL
      type: TYPE_INT32
      json_name: "value"
    }
    options {
      map_entry: true
    }
  }
}
syntax: "proto3"
}
```

As you can see, the compiler created a nested type inside our `Encoding` message called `MEntry` (field name + `Entry`) and it replaced the `map<string, int32>` keyword with a repeated `MEntry` object. With this, we know that maps are effectively syntax sugar for a list of messages.

Knowing that and knowing that repeated complex types are encoded as unpacked repeated, we already know that it will be encoded by interleaving metadata and values. But let's make sure that this is encoded as we think.

We describe the values we want to put in our map in text format (`map/map.txtpb`):

```
m: [
  { key: "1" value: 1 },
  { key: "2" value: 2 }
]
```

Then, we can run the following command:

```
$ cat map.txtpb | protoc --encode=Encoding encoding.proto | hexdump -C
0a 05 0a 01 31 10 01 0a  05 0a 01 32 10 02
```

Our intuition was right. We can see that `0a 05` is repeated for each value. We can also see the encoding of a string (length-delimited) with `0a 01 31` and `0a 01 32`, and we can see the encoding of the int32 value with `10 01` and `10 02`. All of that should feel very familiar now.

So, to conclude, the map has the same overhead we saw when we talked about unpacked repeated fields. However, this has even more overhead than our example regarding a repeated string because here, we have a repeated embedded message. This means that, on top of the duplicated bytes for the m field, we also have duplicated bytes for the fields of the nested message (key and value).

Summary

In this chapter, we learned about all the internal serialization/deserialization algorithms. We saw that there are multiple ways to encode integers and that is why we have that many integer types in Protobuf. After, we covered length-delimited encoding and how it relates to types such as strings, packed repeated fields, and embedded messages. Finally, we talked about unpacked repeated fields and their overhead.

In the next chapter, we will talk about schema evolution over time. We will lean on all the knowledge that we have right now to understand the problems that we might have when updating schemas and how we can overcome them.

Quiz

Answer the following questions to test your knowledge of this chapter:

1. Which encoding algorithm outputs a variable number of bytes depending on the value encoded?

    A. ZigZag

    B. Varint

    C. Length-delimited

2. Which encoding algorithm turns negative numbers into positive ones?

    A. Length-delimited

    B. varint

    C. ZigZag

3. What might be a problem with using varint?

    A. It can use more bytes than the original 32- and 64-bit integers

    B. It will encode negative numbers into 10 bytes

    C. All the above

4. What might be a problem with using ZigZag?

    A. It is less efficient at encoding positive numbers than varint

    B. It will encode negative numbers into 10 bytes

    C. It can use more bytes than the original 32- and 64-bit integers

5. When should you consider using fixed-sized integers?

    A. Never, always prefer using varints

    B. When dealing with larger numbers which will be encoded a more than 4 or 8 bytes

    C. When dealing with negative numbers

6. What is the difference between unpacked and packed repeated fields?

    A. Unpacked has overhead in terms of byte size because it cannot define the length of its items at compile time

    B. Packed has overhead in terms of byte size because it cannot define the length of its items at compile time

Answers

Here are the answers to this chapter's questions:

1. B
2. C
3. C
4. A
5. B
6. A

6

Schema Evolution over Time

Before we enter the practical part of this book, we need to touch on the last important bit about Protobuf. Often, the data schemas evolve and it is important to make sure that newer versions of our app can still interact with older/newer versions of it. Now, while Protobuf does not provide any automatic way of ensuring compatibility between different versions, it provides constructs that can help us.

In this chapter, we're going to cover the following main topics:

- Backward and forward compatibility
- Reserved tags and names
- How to evolve schemas safely

By the end of this chapter, you will understand how to design schemas that are backward and forward compatible, and that are safe to use across versions of your app.

Technical requirements

All the code examples that you will see in this chapter can be found in the `chapter6` directory in this book's GitHub repository (`https://github.com/PacktPublishing/Protocol-Buffers-Handbook`).

Backward and forward compatibility

Backward compatibility is a design that is compatible with older versions of itself. Similarly, forward compatibility is a design that is compatible with newer versions of itself. While this is simple, let's see an example to reinforce the idea.

Backward compatibility

Let's suppose that we have the following schema (proto/v1/id.proto):

```
syntax = "proto3";

message Id {
  uint32 value = 1;
}
```

Previously, this message was doing its job. But after monitoring our use of its values, we noticed that we are getting close to the limit of a uint32 (4,294,967,295). We now need to update the type of value so that it includes more values. But we also need to make sure that previous messages with a uint32 ID are still handled properly.

Let's see what this means by creating a new version of our schema (proto/v2/id.proto):

```
syntax = "proto3";

message Id {
  uint64 value = 1;
}
```

Now, we can define a txtpb file with the following content (proto/v1/id.txtpb):

```
value: 1
```

Then, we can write the encoded binary of this value into a file (v1.out):

```
$ cat proto/v1/id.txtpb | protoc --encode=Id proto/v1/id.proto >
v1.out
$ hexdump -C v1.out
00000000 08 01                                              |..|
00000002
```

Finally, we can read this value into a v2 ID:

```
$ cat v1.out | protoc --decode=Id proto/v2/id.proto
value: 1
```

This proves that we have backward compatibility between v2 and v1. Every message that we serialize in v1 could be deserialized in v2.

Forward compatibility

Now, we can talk about writing a v2 ID and reading that into a v1 ID. If we are testing with the same data (a value of 1), we should have the same output.

We can define a `txtpb` file with the following content (`proto/v2/id.txtpb`):

```
value: 1
```

Then, we can write the encoded binary of this value into a file (`v2.out`):

```
$ cat proto/v2/id.txtpb | protoc --encode=Id proto/v2/id.proto >
v2.out
$ hexdump -C v2.out
00000000 08 01                                            |..|
00000002
```

Finally, we read this into a v1 ID:

```
$ cat v2.out | protoc --decode=Id proto/v1/id.proto
value: 1
```

This proves that we have forward compatibility.

However, if you think about it for a second, we do not have full forward compatibility. uint64 accepts a broader range of numbers than uint32. So, we could have values such as 4,294,967,296, 4,294,967,297, and so on. What would happen in those cases?

Let's work with 4,294,967,297 (`proto/v2/id_overflow.txtpb`):

```
value: 4294967297
```

We can write that to a file:

```
$ cat proto/v2/id_overflow.txtpb | protoc --encode=Id proto/v2/
id.proto > v2_overflow.out
$ hexdump -C v2_overflow.out
00000000   08 81 80 80 80 10                             |......|
00000006
```

Let's try to read that value into a v1 ID:

```
$ cat v2_overflow.out | protoc --decode=Id proto/v1/id.proto
value: 1
```

Here, we have an integer overflow. As we can see in the hexdump output, both values (1 and 4,294,967,297) are not encoded as the same binary. This is what we expect but because of how unsigned numbers are decoded, we get a final value of 1 for both.

Now, note that this problem is not necessarily a Protobuf problem. Our programming languages also have the same behavior. What I am trying to show is that the decoding did not crash and we populated the `value` field. For the question of whether this is good or not, I will let you judge that; however, our applications are still alive and able to communicate.

Some problems

As of now, we only have types that are automatically converted into each other. A uint64 can be converted into a uint32 (with potential overflow) and a uint32 can be converted into a uint64 (not overflow). What happens if we continue our example and change our `Id` field type so that it handles a broader range? For example, what happens if we use a UUID string?

Let's create the v3 schema (`proto/v3/id.proto`):

```
syntax = "proto3";

message Id {
    string value = 1;
}
```

Once again, we create a `txtpb` file but this time with a string value (`proto/v3/id.txtpb`):

```
value: "BA7FAF16-EEB5-477F-B72B-C345F54CB2B4"
```

We write the encoded binary into `v3.out`:

```
$ cat proto/v3/id.txtpb | protoc --encode=Id proto/v3/id.proto >
v3.out
```

Now, we try to decode the `v3.out` binary into a v2 ID:

```
$ cat v3.out | protoc --decode=Id proto/v2/id.proto
1: "BA7FAF16-EEB5-477F-B72B-C345F54CB2B4"
```

Notice that, when we ran the previous protoc decode, we had the field name prefixing the value (for example, a value of 1). However, here, we have the field tag. This means that Protobuf didn't know into which field it should have decoded the value. Yes, they have the same tag (1); however, they do not have a compatible type (integer versus string). Thus, we cannot say that we have forward compatibility in this case because the application in v2 would not receive any value (default value) for the ID.

Once again, notice that this did not crash. We simply have an unknown value decoded. I'm highlighting this one more time because this helps us keep our application alive.

Conclusion

Even though we did not look at the full picture of backward and forward compatibility, we saw that backward compatibility lets you interact with older versions of your app, and forward compatibility lets you interact with newer versions of your app. Furthermore, we saw that some problems might occur during the interaction. However, the important thing that we also talked about is that even though we have problems, the application is not crashing and thus lets us continue the communication.

As mentioned previously, though, we did not look at the full picture for compatibility. We only talked about changing the type of a field and saw how it translates between versions. Now, we need to talk about how we should deal with the problem that we had previously.

Disabling tags – reserved tags

Protobuf has a concept called reserved tags. This means that these tags are made unusable by developers when they are updating a message. This looks like this:

```
message Id {
    reserved 1;
}
```

In this case, tag 1 isn't reusable. This might not be directly clear how, but this helps with the problems that we saw in the previous section. Let's see how.

If you recall the problem of integer overflow, we had a value of 4,294,967,297 encoded and Protobuf, after decoding, returned a value equal to 1. This problem came from the fact that we changed the type of the value field from uint32 to uint64 and we are now trying to encode an uint64 in an uint32. While this did not crash and the `value` field was populated with data, in most cases, we won't want the overflow behavior. This might lead to getting the wrong data for a user, overwriting data that is not from the user, and more.

To prevent this, instead of directly changing the field type (in `v2.proto`), we are going to change the field tag to 2. Now, `v2.proto` looks like this:

```
syntax = "proto3";

message Id {
    uint64 value = 2;
}
```

Let's see what this entails by redoing our writing and reading operations:

```
$ cat proto/v2/id_overflow.txtpb | protoc --encode=Id proto/v2/
id.proto > v2_overflow.out
$ cat v2_overflow.out | protoc --decode=Id proto/v1/id.proto
2: 4294967297
```

We can now see that we get an unknown field with a tag of 2 and a value of 4,294,967,297. This is expected because the value in `v2.proto` has a tag of 2 and it has a tag of 1 in `v1.proto`. Now, this field, because it is unknown, will be skipped, and thus the v1 ID will contain a value with the default value of a uint32 (0).

This also works in the forward compatibility case. If we redo our writing and reading operations for the v1 ID, we get the following:

```
$ cat proto/v1/id.txtpb | protoc --encode=Id proto/v1/id.proto >
v1.out
$ cat v1.out | protoc --decode=Id proto/v2/id.proto
1: 1
```

We also get an unknown field.

While all of this might not be great for the business logic, receiving a default value is still better than receiving an arbitrary number. Now, we can simply handle the default value case, whereas, with an arbitrary value, we could not tell whether it was a normal value or an overflowed one.

We've effectively solved the problem. However, another is arising from what we did. Since we changed the tag from 1 to 2, we released tag 1 for reuse. Any new developer could come in and add a field with a tag of 1. However, this would lead to the problems we talked about previously (overflow, wrong type, and so on).

To avoid this, we must add a reserved tag, like so (`proto/v2/id.proto`):

```
syntax = "proto3";

message Id {
  reserved 1;

  uint64 value = 2;
}
```

We can do the same in `proto/v3/id.proto`:

```
syntax = "proto3";

message Id {
  reserved 1;

  string value = 2;
}
```

This is a protection against the reuse of tag 1 and this makes sure that we have backward and forward compatibility for our message forever, not just temporarily like in the previous example.

Now, notice that our schema reused the name value for both fields (with tags 1 and 2). This might be fine for some simple cases, but it can cause problems at the generated code level for more complex ones. That is why we need reserved names.

Disabling field names – reserved names

> **Important message**
>
> For the sake of simplicity, I will be using Go for this example. If you are not familiar with this language, don't worry. The example is small, and Go is a simple language. I am 100% confident that you can understand what's going on.

We previously saw the need for reserved tags and how they can help with backward and forward compatibility. In this section, we will focus on the impact of the schema's evolution on the code we are writing.

As we know, Protoc is mostly used to generate code out of proto files. This generated code is then used in our application to abstract the Protobuf encoding/decoding. While this is great, this creates some problems when the schemas evolve. Some of these problems can only be solved by going through the code manually and updating it but others are preventable.

Let's see an example of a preventable problem. As you may recall, we now have v1, v2, and v3 of the Id message. They all contain a field named value. However, while the v1 and v2 fields have types that can be converted automatically, v3 breaks our code.

First, we need to add the go_package option to our proto file (proto/v1/id.proto) to tell the protoc compiler in which Go package we would like to generate the code. In my case, the Go module is github.com/PacktPublishing/Protocol-Buffers-Handbook/chapter6 and I have a subdirectory called proto, so I will have the following:

```
syntax = "proto3";

option go_package = "github.com/PacktPublishing/Protocol-Buffers-
Handbook/chapter6/proto";

message Id {
  uint32 value = 1;
}
```

Let's generate the Go code from v1 inside our proto directory:

```
$ protoc --go_out=. --go_opt=module=github.com/PacktPublishing/
Protocol-Buffers-Handbook/chapter6 proto/v1/id.proto
```

This command will take the `go_package` value in `id.proto`, remove the prefix value that's passed into the `go_opt` module (`github.com/PacktPublishing/Protocol-Buffers-Handbook/chapter6`), and generate the source code in the rest of the `go_package` value (proto). Thus, if we list the files and directories in proto, we'll have the following output:

```
$ ls proto
id.pb.go
v1
v2
v3
```

Now, at the root of the project, I can simply create a `main` function that uses the generated code. It looks like this (`main.go`):

```
package main

import "github.com/PacktPublishing/Protocol-Buffers-Handbook/chapter6/
proto"

func main() {
   id := proto.Id{Value: 1}

   println(id.String())
}
```

If we run this, this pretty much does what we expect:

```
$ go run main.go
value:1
```

It prints that `value` is equal to 1.

Now, let's skip v2 and go directly to v3, which is where things break. Remember that the v3 proto file looks like this:

```
syntax = "proto3";

message Id {
   reserved 1;

   string value = 2;
}
```

We changed the type of `value` to `string`.

Let's go through the same steps as before. We'll add our `go_package` to the proto file (`proto/v3/id.proto`):

```
syntax = "proto3";

option go_package = "github.com/PacktPublishing/Protocol-Buffers-
Handbook/chapter6/proto";

message Id {
  reserved 1;

  string value = 2;
}
```

Now, we can generate code in the proto folder:

```
$ protoc --go_out=. --go_opt=module=github.com/PacktPublishing/
Protocol-Buffers-Handbook/chapter6 proto/v3/id.proto
```

Next, let's rerun `main.go`:

```
$ go run main.go
./main.go:6:24: cannot use 1 (untyped int constant) as string value in
struct literal
```

Here, we get an error saying that we are passing an int to a field with a `string` type. And indeed, we are. In `main.go`, we are assigning `value` to `1`. We simply evolved our schema and now our code is breaking at compile time, and we need to update it manually. This might seem trivial because we are in such a small example but try to think about having to go through hundreds of files to update the field. Furthermore, it might not always be obvious how the new value should be set. Should we generate a new UUID? Should we transform the integer into a string?

There are multiple ways of solving this and some of these solutions can only applied to some programming languages. However, Protobuf stays language agnostic and proposes to solve this at the schema level by using reserved names. Let's see what this means.

Instead of having the `value` field in v3 `Id` called `value`, let's call it `uuid` (`proto/v3/id.proto`):

```
syntax = "proto3";

option go_package = "github.com/PacktPublishing/Protocol-Buffers-
Handbook/chapter6/proto";

message Id {
  reserved 1;

  string uuid = 2;
}
```

Now, we can regenerate the code and run `main.go`:

```
$ protoc --go_out=. --go_opt=module=github.com/PacktPublishing/
Protocol-Buffers-Handbook/chapter6 proto/v3/id.proto
$ go run main.go
./main.go:6:17: unknown field Value in struct literal of type "github.
com/PacktPublishing/Protocol-Buffers-Handbook/chapter6/proto".Id
```

We still get an error. However, this time, we do not have any way of passing values that are potentially correct for the type but incorrect in our app. Here, the field simply does not exist, and this protects us from implicit conversions between types.

Now, once again, a new programmer could come and add a field called `value` and we would come back to our problematic state of potentially having implicit conversions since the field now exists. To solve this problem, we can simply reserve the name, like so:

```
syntax = "proto3";

option go_package = "github.com/PacktPublishing/Protocol-Buffers-
Handbook/chapter6/proto";

message Id {
  reserved 1;
  reserved "value";

  string uuid = 2;
}
```

With this, our code will never see a `value` field for future versions.

As you can see, this is more like protection for the code. This is because, as you may recall, names are not encoded in the binary, only tags and types are. We saw encoding/decoding safety with reserved tags and now, we have code safety with reserved names.

The evolution rules

We saw multiple problems caused by the evolution of the proto file and it is important to keep these in mind. So, it is time to recapitulate and formulate rules on how to evolve schemas in Protobuf.

Here's the list of rules that we should follow if we need to maintain backward and forward compatibility:

- **Never remove a reserved statement**. This probably goes without saying but reserved statements are here to protect us. Do not remove or modify them; otherwise, you will get undefined behaviors.

- **Never modify a field tag**. This will lead Protobuf to decode data into unknown fields between versions. This means you will not receive that data and get a default value.

- **Avoid reusing a field tag**. As we saw, this can cause problems such as integer overflow or other problems due to type conversion. It is better to just add a new field to deal with the new data. Remember that tags are encoded as varints.

- **Always add a reserved tag when deleting a field**. This prevents newer versions from accidentally reusing that tag and thus leads to the problems mentioned in the previous point.

- **Consider adding a reserved name**. This is optional but this might have a good long-term impact on the code you are writing. As we saw, this can prevent the reuse of field names and protect against implicit conversions.

- **Consider making packages named after versions**. We did not talk about this during this chapter, but we could package each version with a version name (for example, package v3). This would lead developers to be more explicit about which version of the message they are using.

To conclude, if backward and forward compatibility are important for you, think about the interaction between the different versions of your app. Protobuf provides great ways to help you securely update your schema, but it is important that you first identify the problem you might have. Protobuf is not going to solve that for you automatically.

Summary

In this chapter, we saw the problems that might be created by evolving our schemas and how to solve each of them. We also derived a set of rules that we can follow when we are in the process of such evolution. This concludes the "theoretical" part of this book, which means we can confidently go to the practical part.

In the next chapter, we are going to create a CLI application in Go for an address book where the data is serialized and deserialized with Protobuf. This will help us practice the Protobuf syntax, the use of protoc, and the use of its generated code.

Quiz

Answer the following questions to test your knowledge of this chapter:

1. What is backward compatibility?

    A. The ability to interact with newer versions of our app

    B. The ability to interact with older versions of our app

2. What is forward compatibility?

    A. The ability to interact with newer versions of our app

    B. The ability to interact with older versions of our app

3. Would there be any backward compatibility problem if, instead of changing the field type from uint32 to uint64, we were changing from uint64 to uint32?

    A. Yes, we might have an overflow

    B. No, all uint32 values are included in uint64

4. Would there be any forward compatibility problem if, instead of changing the field type from uint32 to uint64, we were changing from uint64 to uint32?

    A. Yes, we might have an overflow

    B. No, all uint32 values are included in uint64

5. What could potentially happen if we changed a field type from int32 to uint64 (hint: think in both forward and backward compatibility terms)?

    A. Negative values will be encoded as a large number

    B. Values bigger than MAX_INT32 will overflow

    C. All of the above

6. When should you use a reserved tag?

    A. When you change the type of a field

    B. When you change the name of a field

    C. When you remove a field

7. When should you consider using a reserved name?

    A. When you change the type of a field

    B. When you change the name of a field

    C. When you remove a field

Answers

Here are the answers to this chapter's questions:

1. B
2. A
3. B
4. A
5. C
6. C
7. B and/or C

7

Implementing the Address Book in Go

From this chapter on, we are going to see a more practical use of Protobuf. In earlier chapters, we talked about syntax, how to carefully craft schema, and how to generate code from these schemas. We will now use the generated code in a programming language to create a local address book in which we can store and list contacts.

In this chapter, we're going to cover the following main topics:

- Interacting with most Protobuf constructs in Go

- Writing/reading Protobuf encoded data to/from a file

- Using Protobuf reflection to act on field data

By the end of the chapter, you will be able to interact with Protobuf-generated code in Go. You will understand how to use the generated code in your application to serialize and deserialize any kind of data.

Technical requirements

All the code that you will see in this chapter can be found in the directory called `chapter7` in the GitHub repository (`https://github.com/PacktPublishing/Protocol-Buffers-Handbook`).

> Disclaimer
> This chapter will focus on the Go implementation of an address book. This is in no way a Go tutorial, so if you are not familiar with the language and do not want to go through this, you can find a Python implementation in the next chapter. However, I would still encourage you to skim through this chapter to be able to analyze the difference between the generated Go code and the Python code. You will see that Protobuf generates idiomatic code, and some concepts have different feels in different languages.

The project: address book

As mentioned in the introduction, this is a practical chapter. We are going to create a mini **command-line interface (CLI)** that lets us create and list contacts in an address book. Before we dive into the code, we will talk about the project itself and some of the architectural choices made in this project.

So, let's talk about the project. This address book project was heavily influenced by the official tutorial in the Protobuf documentation (`https://protobuf.dev/getting-started/gotutorial/`). However, there are quite a few changes that I made to cover more Protobuf concepts. Here are the changes that I made:

- Instead of adding only a person's contact in the address book, we will also be able to add a company's contact. This lets us use `oneof` because the contact will be either a company or a person.

- While the CLI will not cover searching the contact by name (this is a challenge for you), we made sure that it would be possible to do so. Instead of having a list of contacts, we have a `map` of strings to contact.

- For the sake of readability, we removed some of the extra fields that we did not need for this example to simplify the code a bit.

In other words, the goal of this project is to use as many concepts as possible provided by Protobuf in a simple but interesting project.

Now, as mentioned, this project is a CLI. It is going to have two commands. The add command will support the following flags:

- `name`: This is the contact's name.
- `kind`: This is either `cie`, `company`, `per`, or `person`. It denotes what kind of contact we are adding.
- `email`: This is the contact's email.
- `dep`: This is the contact's department. It is only used for company contacts and is ignored otherwise. It can take the values `hr` (human resources) or `cs` (customer service).
- `phone`: This is the contact's phone number.
- `type`: The type (for person) or department (for company) of phone number. It can take the values `home`, `mobile`, or `work`.

For example, we can add a person, with the email address `test@test.com` and the mobile phone `11111111`, like so:

```
$ ./addressbook add -name "Clément" -kind "per" -phone "11111111"
-type "mobile" -email test@test.com
```

The `list` command will not support any flags just yet. However, once called, it will display contact information on the screen. For the previously added contact, we would get the following:

```
./addressbook list
name: Clément
last_updated: 03/08/2024 07:24:55
person: {
  email: "test@test.com"
  phones: {
    number: "11111111"
    type: TYPE_MOBILE
  }
}
---------------------------
```

You can see all the information that we are storing. On top of the data provided in flags, we also display the last updated time. This lets us use a Well-Known type called `Timestamp`.

Finally, all the information is stored in a file called `addressbook.db`. If it does not exist on the first `addressbook add`, it will be created and filled out.

The last thing important to mention is the project's architecture. The final project will have the following folder structure

```
.
├── cmd
│   └── addressbook
│       ├── add.go
│       ├── addressbook.go
│       └── list.go
├── go.mod
├── main.go
├── pkg
│   └── addressbook
│       ├── add.go
│       ├── addressbook.go
│       └── list.go
└── proto
    └── addressbook.proto
```

The most important thing to note is that we separate the business logic from the command line part of this application. All of this should be familiar to you if you have worked on a CLI in Go. The handling of flags, the opening/closing of the database, and basic flag validation will be handled in the respective go file in the cmd package. The creation and serialization/deserialization of contact will be handled in the pkg package. Finally, the Protobuf schema and the generated code will live in the proto package.

Now that we know what how project is and how we are going to organize it, let's jump into it.

Defining the schema

Starting a project involving Protobuf always starts by defining the schema. This is known as **Schema-Driven Development (SDD)**. We essentially define the contract that needs to be fulfilled.

We are going to take a bottom-up approach to design this schema. We are going to start by defining what a `Person` contact looks like. As we saw in the description of the project, a person can have an email and multiple phone numbers. This looks like the following (`proto/addressbook.proto`):

```
message Person {
  //...
  string email = 1;
  repeated PhoneNumber phones = 2;
}
```

While the email is simply a string, the phone number will be represented by a nested message. This is because we want to be able to store the phone number and the type of phone number it is. As we know, the type of phone number can be mobile, work, or home. This means that we can represent this set of values with an enum. Knowing all of this, we now have the following:

```
message Person {
  message PhoneNumber {
    enum Type {
      TYPE_UNSPECIFIED = 0;
      TYPE_MOBILE = 1;
      TYPE_HOME = 2;
      TYPE_WORK = 3;
    }

    string number = 1;
    Type type = 2;
  }

  //email + phones
}
```

Hopefully, all of this should look very familiar now.

Now, let us go with the message for a Company contact. This will be very similar to what we did with the Person message; however, in this case, we will have the possibility to add multiple phone numbers and emails with a respective company Department. This means that we are going to have two lists, one for storing the EmailAddress type and the other for storing the PhoneNumber type:

```
message Company {
  //...
  repeated EmailAddress emails = 1;
  repeated PhoneNumber phones = 2;
}
```

The EmailAddress type will contain the email address and the Department related to that address:

```
message Company {
  message EmailAddress {
    string email = 1;
    Department department = 2;
  }
  //...
}
```

Similarly, the PhoneNumber type stores the number and its department:

```
message Company {
  message PhoneNumber {
    string number = 1;
    Department department = 2;
  }
  //...
}
```

And finally, Department will simply be an enum that lists all the departments available:

```
message Company {
  enum Department {
    DEPARTMENT_UNSPECIFIED = 0;
    DEPARTMENT_HR = 1;
    DEPARTMENT_CUSTOMER_SERVICE = 2;
  }
  //...
}
```

Next, we need to design a `Contact`. As we know, a contact can be a `Person` or a `Company`. This means we can use a `oneof` since we want to make sure that the data is mutually exclusive. Thus, we have the following:

```
message Contact {
  //...
  oneof kind {
    Person person = 2;
    Company company = 3;
  }
}
```

And, if you remember, we will also store the last updated time for the contact entry. For this, we will use the `google.protobuf.Timestamp` Well-Known Type. This looks like the following:

```
import "google/protobuf/timestamp.proto";

message Contact {
  google.protobuf.Timestamp last_updated = 1;
  //...
}
```

Finally, we need to represent the `AddressBook` itself. As mentioned, we want to be able to map a contact name to the contact entry. Thus, we will use a map of string (names) to `Contact`. The `AddressBook` is as simple as this:

```
message AddressBook {
  map<string, Contact> contacts = 1;
}
```

The only thing left to us is to define the package into which the generated code will be written. For this, we use a Golang-specific file option called `go_package`. In our case, we want the generated code in the `proto` package, thus, at the top of the file after the syntax and import, we have the following statement:

```
syntax = "proto3";

import "google/protobuf/timestamp.proto";

option go_package = "github.com/PacktPublishing/Protocol-Buffers-
Handbook/chapter7/proto";
```

Notice that `github.com/PacktPublishing/Protocol-Buffers-Handbook/chapter7` is the name of the Go module, and `proto` is the directory inside this module. This might be different for you, depending on your Go module name.

That is pretty much it for the schema. Let's make sure that we generate the code before continuing. We will use the `--go_out` and the `--go_opt=paths` flags that we saw in the chapter on Protobuf compiler (*Chapter 4*). We execute the following:

```
$ protoc --go_out=. --go_opt=paths=source_relative proto/addressbook.proto
```

In the end, we should have the following files in the `proto` directory:

```
proto
├── addressbook.pb.go
└── addressbook.proto
```

We just generated our code! We are now ready to move on and start tackling the main part of our application: the adding of entries. However, before we dive into that, we will need a few helper functions to read/write from/to files and convert a string (passed by command line) into a `PhoneNumber` `Type` or a `Company Department`.

Boilerplate code

Let's prepare some convenient helpers for the journey ahead. We know we will need writing/reading to/from files and that we will need to transform some arguments, passed as strings, into Go types. Let's deal with the latter first since this is a very trivial task.

Converting string to enum values

We are going to create two functions: `strToPhoneType` and `strToDepartment`. They look similar since we are going to check the value of the string and derive an enum value from it. Let's start with `strToPhoneType`.

We know that the `PhoneType` enum contains the values `TYPE_HOME`, `TYPE_MOBILE`, `TYPE_WORK`, and `TYPE_UNSPECIFIED`. `TYPE_UNSPECIFIED` is the default value of `PhoneType` since enums have 0 as their default value. Conveniently, Golang initializes variables with 0 values. Thus, we will simply check for the values of `home`, `mobile`, and `work`. If the string does not contain anything or a value that isn't one of these, the phone type will be considered unspecified. The **pseudocode** for `strToPhoneType` looks like the following:

```
func strToPhoneType(str string) Type {
  var t Type

  switch str {
  case "home":
    t = TYPE_HOME
  case "mobile":
```

```
    t = TYPE_MOBILE
  case "work":
    t = TYPE_WORK
  }

  return t
}
```

Now, we need to look at the generated code to make this function compile and create PhoneNumber Type. If we take a look at `proto/addressbook.pb.go`, we can see that we have a type called Person_PhoneNumber_Type, which is an alias for `int32` and some constant values using that type:

```
type Person_PhoneNumber_Type int32

const (
  Person_PhoneNumber_TYPE_UNSPECIFIED  Person_PhoneNumber_Type = 0
  Person_PhoneNumber_TYPE_MOBILE   Person_PhoneNumber_Type = 1
  Person_PhoneNumber_TYPE_HOME   Person_PhoneNumber_Type = 2
  Person_PhoneNumber_TYPE_WORK   Person_PhoneNumber_Type = 3
)
```

You can see that the generated type is named after the different nested messages. If you remember, Person is the parent of PhoneNumber and PhoneNumber is the parent of the Type enum.

Now that we know the name of the type and its possible values, let's make the previous pseudocode correct for our Go compiler. It looks like this (`pkg/addressbook/addressbook.go`):

```
import (
  pb "github.com/PacktPublishing/Protocol-Buffers-Handbook/chapter7/
  proto"
)

func strToPhoneType(str string) pb.Person_PhoneNumber_Type {
  var t pb.Person_PhoneNumber_Type

  switch str {
  case "home":
    t = pb.Person_PhoneNumber_TYPE_HOME
  case "mobile":
    t = pb.Person_PhoneNumber_TYPE_MOBILE
  case "work":
    t = pb.Person_PhoneNumber_TYPE_WORK
  }
```

```
    return t
}
```

Now, it is not hard to imagine what the Department type will look like. Since we know that Department is an enum inside the message called Company, the type will be called Company_Department. And indeed, if we look at the generated code, we have (proto/addressbook.pb.go):

```
type Company_Department int32

const (
  Company_DEPARTMENT_UNSPECIFIED Company_Department = 0
  Company_DEPARTMENT_HR Company_Department = 1
  Company_DEPARTMENT_CUSTOMER_SERVICE Company_Department = 2
)
```

So, similarly to strToPhoneType, we can create a switch and derive the Department value from the string value (pkg/addressbook/addressbook.go):

```
func strToDepartment(str string) pb.Company_Department {
  var d pb.Company_Department

  switch str {
  case "hr":
    d = pb.Company_DEPARTMENT_HR
  case "cs":
    d = pb.Company_DEPARTMENT_CUSTOMER_SERVICE
  }

  return d
}
```

While this was a pretty trivial task, this needed to be done and during this process, we took our first look at the generated code. We learned that the name of the generated type is given by the concatenation of the nested types' names separated by an underscore. Let's now focus on reading an address book from the database file.

Reading/writing from/to a file

The core of the application relies on the **input/output (I/O)** operations that are reading from the file and writing to the file. Each time we add a new contact, we will need to first read the AddressBook, then add the contact to it, and finally, write the AddressBook back to the file. Let's start by reading from the file.

First of all, we know that we will return an AddressBook or an error. This is easy to do in Go; we can simply write the following (pkg/addressbook/addressbook.go):

```
func readFromDb(...) (*pb.AddressBook, error) {
  //...
}
```

Next, we need to think about how we are going to receive the file or file path as an argument. We could simply receive a string being the path of the file. We could also receive an os.File struct to simply represent the file and read from it. While both are fine, I decided to go with a more generic approach: using io.Reader.

There are two reasons for choosing this interface. The first one is that I was able to test the functionality of the functions using readFromDb with a fake implementation of a Database. If this seems interesting to you, take a look at the FakeDb type in the pkg/addressbook/addressbook_test.go file.

The second reason is that we are in the business logic of our application (pkg/addressbook) and thus we do not want to be tied to specific storage. By having this interface, we could easily reuse readFromDb with a different storage. For example, we could be reading from the network.

Thus, we now have this:

```
import (
  "io"

  //...
)

func readFromDb(db io.Reader) (*pb.AddressBook, error) {
  //...
)
```

Next, we are going to read the whole content from the reader into memory. For a small application like ours, this will be fine. We do not need to care about buffering and reading into chunks:

```
func readFromDb(db io.Reader) (*pb.AddressBook, error) {
  in, err := io.ReadAll(db)
  if err != nil {
    return nil, err
```

```
    }
    //...
}
```

And finally, now that we have the bytes out of the file, we can use a function provided by the Protobuf standard library called Unmarshal. It takes some bytes and tries to deserialize the data into a type. In our case, we will deserialize the bytes into an AddressBook:

```
import (
  //...
  "google.golang.org/protobuf/proto"
)

func readFromDb(db io.Reader) (*pb.AddressBook, error) {
  //...

  var book pb.AddressBook
  if err = proto.Unmarshal(in, &book); err != nil {
    return nil, err
  }
  return &book, err
}
```

This is as simple as this; we created a function that takes bytes from an io.Reader and turns them into a Protobuf-generated type.

The writeToDb function is similar to the readFromDb function. However, instead of using io.Reader, we will use io.Writer, and instead of using Unmarshal, we will use Marshal. The function looks like this:

```
func writeToDb(db io.Writer, book *pb.AddressBook) error {
  out, err := proto.Marshal(book)
  if err != nil {
    return err
  }

  if _, err = db.Write(out); err != nil {
    return err
  }
  return nil
}
```

We now have all the boilerplate code needed to go ahead. We will now focus on adding entries to an AddressBook and writing it to a file.

Adding entries

In this section, let's focus on adding a Person or a Company contact to the AddressBook. We will start with the business logic (pkg) and then we will link the business logic to the CLI part of our application (cmd).

The business logic

We will first add a new file under pkg/addressbook called add.go. This will contain all the code related to the addition of contact. In this file, we will have two functions: AddPerson and AddCompany. These functions are similar; however, they receive different information as parameters. Let's first talk about the similarities between these two functions.

The first similarity is that both functions take db as a parameter. Once again, we will use an interface to keep this code as generic as possible. This time, however, we will use the io.ReadWriter interface since we need both Read and Write functions. So, we have the following (pkg/addressbook/add.go):

```go
func AddPerson(db io.ReadWriter, ...) error {
  //...
}

func AddCompany(db io.ReadWriter, ...) error {
  //...
}
```

Next, both functions will use readFromDb to get the potentially already existing serialized data, and then writeToDb to save the newly updated data. Both functions will contain the following beginning and ending:

```go
{
  book, err := readFromDb(db)
  if err != nil {
    return err
  }

  if book.Contacts == nil {
    book.Contacts = make(map[string]*pb.Contact)
  }
  contact, ok := book.Contacts[name]

  //...

  if err = writeToDb(db, book); err != nil {
```

```
        return err
    }
    return nil
}
```

Firstly, notice that we have a `name` variable in this example. This will be passed as the string in the parameters of the functions. We will see that soon. Secondly, notice that we are initializing `book`. `Contacts` with a new map since, in Go, maps are nil initialized and the first time we create the `db` file there will be no `Contacts` data. Other than that, the code should be self-explanatory.

Now, let's get into the difference between the two add functions. These differences mostly come from the fact that we are dealing with two different types. If we look at the generated code, we can find the following types (`proto/addressbook.pb.go`):

```
type Person struct {
    Email   string
    Phones  []*Person_PhoneNumber
}

type Company struct {
    Emails  []*Company_EmailAddress
    Phones  []*Company_PhoneNumber
}
```

But the most important thing that you need to notice is the code generated for `Contact` and the `oneof` we used. We have the following:

```
type Contact struct {
    LastUpdated *timestamppb.Timestamp
    // Types that are assignable to Kind:
    //
    // *Contact_Person
    // *Contact_Company
    Kind isContact_Kind
}

type isContact_Kind interface {
    isContact_Kind()
}

type Contact_Person struct {
    Person *Person
}
```

```
type Contact_Company struct {
  Company *Company
}


func (*Contact_Person) isContact_Kind() {}
func (*Contact_Company) isContact_Kind() {}
```

We can see that Contact.Kind is of type isContact_Kind, which is an interface that is implemented by both Contact_Person and Contact_Company. This means that when we are going to set the Kind field, we will need to provide it with Contact_Person or Contact_Company, which are wrappers around Person and Company. This also means that when we read the data from the db, we will need to cast isContact_Kind to a concrete implementation. So, for AddPerson, this will look like this:

```
func AddPerson(db io.ReadWriter, ...) error {
  //...

  var person *pb.Person

  if ok { // contact already exists
    person = contact.Kind.(*pb.Contact_Person).Person
  } else { // contact does not exist
    person = &pb.Person{}
  }

  //...
}
```

And similarly, for AddCompany, it will look like this:

```
func AddCompany(db io.ReadWriter, ...) error {
  //...
  var cie *pb.Company

  if ok { // contact already exists
    cie = contact.Kind.(*pb.Contact_Company).Company
  } else { // contact does not exist
    cie = &pb.Company{}
  }
  //...
}
```

What is left is handling the data that we will get as parameters and adding it to the AddressBook. As we know, for the Person we will need a name, an email, a phone number, and a phone type.

As of now, we will consider that the name is never empty because we are going to check that in the cmd package. However, we cannot assume that the email, phone number, and phone type are not empty. So, depending on whether the data exists, we are going to update Person or Company. For AddPerson, this will look like the following:

```
func AddPerson(db io.ReadWriter, name, email, phoneNb, phoneType
string) error {
  //...
  if len(email) != 0 {
    person.Email = email
  }

  if len(phoneNb) != 0 {
    person.Phones = append(person.Phones, &pb.Person_PhoneNumber{
      Number: phoneNb,
      Type:   strToPhoneType(phoneType),
    })
  }
  //...
}
```

For AddCompany, it will look similar to the Phones field in the AddPerson, but we handle departments instead of types:

```
func AddCompany(db io.ReadWriter, name, email, emailDep, phoneNb,
phoneDep string) error {
  //...
  if len(email) != 0 {
    cie.Emails = append(cie.Emails, &pb.Company_EmailAddress{
      Email:      email,
      Department: strToDepartment(emailDep),
    })
  }

  if len(phoneNb) != 0 {
    cie.Phones = append(cie.Phones, &pb.Company_PhoneNumber{
      Number:     phoneNb,
      Department: strToDepartment(phoneDep),
    })
  }
  //...
}
```

The main thing to note in these two code snippets is that we are appending to Phones and Emails. This is because we want to be able to add another phone number or email to an existing contact. If the contact already exists, we simply add the new info at the end of the contact's lists.

Finally, we simply need to create/recreate a Contact to override the information in AddressBook. Contacts[name]. While we could check once again if the contact already exists and update accordingly, for the sake of brevity, we will simply create a new Contact every time. For AddPerson, we have the following:

```go
import (
    //...
    "google.golang.org/protobuf/types/known/timestamppb"
)


func AddPerson(db io.ReadWriter, name, email, phoneNb, phoneType
string) error {
    //...
    book.Contacts[name] = &pb.Contact{
        LastUpdated: timestamppb.Now(),
        Kind: &pb.Contact_Person{
            Person: person,
        },
    }
    //...
}
```

And for AddCompany, we have the following:

```go
func AddCompany(db io.ReadWriter, name, email, emailDep, phoneNb,
phoneDep string) error {
    //...
    book.Contacts[name] = &pb.Contact{
        LastUpdated: timestamppb.Now(),
        Kind: &pb.Contact_Company{
            Company: cie,
        },
    }
    //...
}
```

Notice the use of the function called Now in the timestamppb package. This is a function that creates a Timestamp (a Well-Known Type provided by Protobuf) from the current time. If you are familiar with the time package from the Go standard library and its Now function, this is pretty much the same.

Believe it or not, the business logic of adding contacts to our AddressBook is finished. We have created a way to take raw information (strings), create and update a contact, and serialize/deserialize data from the database. We can now focus on integrating that with the CLI part of our application.

The CLI

> **Important note**
>
> This section is here for the sake of completeness and is not related to using Protobuf in Go. It is mostly binding the business logic to the CLI part of the application. Feel free to skip this part if you are not working on the AddressBook project.

Since we have the business logic for adding entries, the only thing left to do for the add command is to create the user interface. To do that, we are going to create the parsing and validation of command-line arguments. Let's start with the validation.

In our application, we need to make sure that a few things are consistent before passing them along to the business logic. For example, the name of the contact should never be empty since this is the main information we use to store the contact in the AddressBook.Contacts map. Thus, a function should check all the potential problems and return an error to the user. We are going to do this in a function called addContact in the cmd/addressbook package in a file called add.go.

For now, we can start with the following:

```go
import (
  "fmt"
  "io"
  "os"
)

func addContact(db io.ReadWriter, name, kind string, ...) {
  if len(name) == 0 {
    fmt.Println("contact name cannot be empty.")
    os.Exit(1)
  }

  if len(kind) == 0 {
    fmt.Println("contact kind cannot be empty.")
    os.Exit(1)
  }
  //...
}
```

Now, as we saw before, the different `add` instances are receiving different information. However, here, we will receive all the possible information and derive which business logic function to call. If the kind is `per` or `person`, we will call the `AddPerson` function, and if the kind is `cie` or `company`, we will call the `AddCompany` function. We now have the following:

```go
import (
  //...

  "github.com/PacktPublishing/Protocol-Buffers-Handbook/chapter7/pkg/
  addressbook"
)

func addContact(db io.ReadWriter, name, kind, email, emailDep,
phoneNb, phoneType string) {
  //...
  switch kind {
  case "per", "person":
    if err := addressbook.AddCompany(db, name, email, emailDep,
    phoneNb, phoneType); err != nil {
      fmt.Printf("error: %s\n", err)
      os.Exit(1)
    }
  case "cie", "company":
    if err := addressbook.AddPerson(db, name, email, phoneNb,
    phoneType); err != nil {
      fmt.Printf("error: %s\n", err)
      os.Exit(1)
    }
  default:
    fmt.Println("unknown kind", kind)
    os.Exit(1)
  }
}
```

The only thing left to do to let the users use our add feature is to parse the command-line arguments and call `addContact` if the subcommand is "add". This will be done in a function called `Execute` in cmd/addressbook/addressbook.go. This function will then be called from the main.go at the root of the repository so that we can simply execute go run easily. Let us start with `Execute`.

In this function, we will parse the command-line arguments, open the database file, and call the `addContact` function. This looks like the following:

```go
import (
  "flag"
  "fmt"
```

```go
    "os"
)

const (
    dbFilePath = "addressbook.db"
)

func Execute() {
    addCmd := flag.NewFlagSet("add", flag.ExitOnError)
    name := addCmd.String("name", "", "the contact's name.")
    kind := addCmd.String("kind", "", "the kind of contact (company or
    person).")
    email := addCmd.String("email", "", "the contact's email.")
    emailDep := addCmd.String("dep", "", "the contact's department.")
    phoneNb := addCmd.String("phone", "", "the contact's phone number.")
    phoneType := addCmd.String("type", "", "the type of phone number.")

    if len(os.Args) < 2 {
        fmt.Println("expected 'add' or 'list' subcommands")
        os.Exit(1)
    }

    db, err := os.OpenFile(dbFilePath, os.O_RDWR|os.O_CREATE, 0600)
    if err != nil {
        fmt.Printf("error: %s", err)
        os.Exit(1)
    }
    defer db.Close()

    switch os.Args[1] {
    case "add":
        addCmd.Parse(os.Args[2:])
        addContact(db, *name, *kind, *email, *emailDep, *phoneNb,
        *phoneType)
    case "list":
        //TBD


    default:
        fmt.Println("expected 'add' or 'list' subcommands")
        os.Exit(1)
    }
}
```

And now, in `main.go`, we can simply write the following:

```
import "github.com/PacktPublishing/Protocol-Buffers-Handbook/chapter7/
cmd/addressbook"

func main() {
   addressbook.Execute()
}
```

This is it! We have our first command in the CLI. To try it, we can simply pass arguments at the end. For example, if we wanted to add a `Person`, we would execute this:

```
$ go run main.go add -name "Clément" -kind "per" -phone "11111111"
-type "mobile" -email test@test.com
```

And if we wanted to add a company, we would run this:

```
$ go run main.go add -name "Google" -kind "cie" -phone "11111111"
-type "hr" -email cs.test@test.com -dep "cs"
```

If you try to run these commands, you will notice that a file called `addressbook.db` has been created. This is where the data has been serialized. However, if you look at the data inside, you will see that it is binary. We need a better way to take a look at this data and this is why we need the list command.

Listing entries

The business logic

The job left for CLI to be completed is rather small. We only need to read data from the database and display it on the standard output. Let's start by reading the data from the database (`pkg/addressbook/list.go`):

```
import (
   "io"
)

func ListContacts(db io.Reader, ...) error {
   book, err := readFromDb(db)
   if err != nil {
     return err
   }
   //...
}
```

Next, we can order the list of contacts alphabetically. This was mostly done for testing purposes, but it could be used for more advanced features, such as filtering or paging. Here, we will simply focus on displaying all the contacts. The sorting looks like the following:

```
import (
  //...
  "sort"
)

func ListContacts(db io.Reader, w io.Writer, redact bool) error {
  //...
  names := make([]string, 0, len(book.Contacts))
  for name := range book.Contacts {
    names = append(names, name)
  }
  sort.Strings(names)
  //...
}
```

Now that we have sorted names, we can just loop over them and display the information:

```
import (
  //...
  "fmt"

  "google.golang.org/protobuf/encoding/prototext"
)

func ListContacts(db io.Reader, w io.Writer) error {
  //...
  for _, name := range names {
    contact := book.Contacts[name]
    time := contact.LastUpdated.AsTime()
    contact.LastUpdated = nil
    fmt.Fprintf(w, "name: %s\n", name)
    fmt.Fprintf(w, "last_updated: %s\n", time.Format("01/02/2006
    15:04:05"))
    fmt.Fprintf(w, "%s", prototext.Format(contact))
    fmt.Fprintln(w, "---------------------")
  }
  return nil
}
```

There are a few things to notice here. The first one is that we are using `Fprintf` to print on the Writer. Once again, we are trying to keep the code as generic as possible in the business logic. This lets us choose in the CLI application where to write the information.

Next, you can see that we are using the `AsTime` function on `LastUpdated`. If you remember, we used the `timestamppb.Now()` function to create a `google.protobuf.Timestamp` well-known type from a Go time. This is the opposite. We are taking a Timestamp and turning it into a Go time.

Finally, you can see that we are setting the `LastUpdated` to nil. This is entirely for aesthetic reasons. Later in the code, we use the `prototext.Format` function, which shows the Protobuf data in Protobuf text format. We simply do not want the `LastUpdated` data to be displayed like this because it would show the internals of the `Timestamp` type. We simply want a beautiful date/time printed on the screen.

That is it for the business logic. Let's now switch to the CLI part of the feature.

The CLI

> **Important note**
>
> This section is here for the sake of completeness and is not related to using Protobuf in Go; it is mostly binding the business logic to the CLI part of the application. Feel free to skip this part if you are not working on the `AddressBook` project.

Similarly to what we did for `addContact`, we will create a `listContacts` function that will call the business logic function and exit when there's an error. In `cmd/addressbook/list.go`, we will have the following:

```go
import (
  "fmt"
  "io"
  "os"

  "github.com/PacktPublishing/Protocol-Buffers-Handbook/chapter7/pkg/
  addressbook"
)

func listContacts(db io.Reader) {
  if err := addressbook.ListContacts(db, os.Stdout); err != nil {
    fmt.Printf("error: %s\n", err)
    os.Exit(1)
  }
}
```

Finally, we will handle the command-line parsing. We do not have any arguments yet, but we will have them in the next section. In `cmd/addressbook/addressbook.go`, we will add the following code to `Execute`:

```
func Execute() {
  // addCmd

  listCmd := flag.NewFlagSet("list", flag.ExitOnError)

  if len(os.Args) < 2 {
    fmt.Println("expected 'add' or 'list' subcommands")
    os.Exit(1)
  }

  // db

  switch os.Args[1] {
  // add
  case "list":
    listCmd.Parse(os.Args[2:])
    listContacts(db)
  // default
  }
}
```

And just like that, we now have the list subcommand in our CLI.

Let's try that by first adding some data to our `AddressBook`:

```
$ go run main.go add -name "Clément" -kind "per" -phone "11111111"
-type "mobile" -email test@test.com
```

And then, we can see the serialized data by running the following:

```
$ go run main.go list
name: Clément
last_updated: 03/11/2024 01:07:37
person: {
  email: "test@test.com"
  phones: {
    number: "11111111"
    type: TYPE_MOBILE
  }
}
```

As expected, we get the name, a formatted time, and all the information on the person.

Hiding sensitive data

The last thing that I want to add for this mini-project to be complete is to work with a `field` option. In our case, we will work with an option called `debug_redact`. This tells an application to redact the private information in the data. For us, this means hiding the phone numbers and email addresses.

Let's start by adding the option to the fields we want to redact in our `proto` file:

```
message Person {
  //...
  message PhoneNumber {
    string number = 1 [debug_redact = true];
    Type type = 2;
  }

  string email = 1 [debug_redact = true];
  repeated PhoneNumber phones = 2;
}

message Company {
  //...
  message EmailAddress {
    string email = 1 [debug_redact = true];
    Department department = 2;
  }

  message PhoneNumber {
    string number = 1 [debug_redact = true];
    Department department = 2;
  }
  //...
}
```

Next, as always, we need to compile the schema to generate the code out of it. We run the following command:

```
$ protoc --go_out=. --go_opt=paths=source_relative proto/addressbook.proto
```

Next, we need a helper function to loop over the fields of a message, detect this option, and edit the information in the field. To do this, we are going to use Protobuf reflection. In `pkg/addressbook/addressbook.go`, we are going to create a function called `redactPrivateInfo`. It looks like the following:

```
import (
  //...
```

```
     "google.golang.org/protobuf/proto"
  )

  func redactPrivateInfo(msg proto.Message) {
    //...
  }
```

Next, to use Protobuf reflection, we need to call the `ProtoReflect` function on the message. It will return a `protoreflect.Message` (https://pkg.go.dev/google.golang.org/protobuf/reflect/protoreflect#Message), which is an interface that provides the Range function to iterate over populated fields. We now have the following:

```
  import (
    //...
    "google.golang.org/protobuf/reflect/protoreflect"
  )

  func redactPrivateInfo(msg proto.Message) {
    m := msg.ProtoReflect()
    m.Range(func(fd protoreflect.FieldDescriptor, v protoreflect.Value)
    bool {
      //...
      return true
    })
  }
```

From the `FieldDescriptor` (`fd`), we can then get the `FieldOptions` by calling the `Options` function and casting the result to `*descriptorpb.FieldOptions` (https://pkg.go.dev/google.golang.org/protobuf/types/descriptorpb#FieldOptions). Then, if the cast succeeds and we can find the debug_redact option, we will redact the data. This looks like the following:

```
  func redactPrivateInfo(msg proto.Message) {
    m := msg.ProtoReflect()
    m.Range(func(fd protoreflect.FieldDescriptor, v protoreflect.Value)
    bool {
      opts := fd.Options().(*descriptorpb.FieldOptions)
      if opts != nil && *opts.DebugRedact {
        //...
      }
      return true
    })
  }
```

Finally, let's replace the data of the strings with a series of asterisks. We will check if the kind of data the field contains is a string and if that is the case, we will set the value to a string containing the same number of asterisks as the number of characters in the original string. We now have this:

```go
func redactPrivateInfo(msg proto.Message) {
  m := msg.ProtoReflect()
  m.Range(func(fd protoreflect.FieldDescriptor, v protoreflect.Value)
  bool {
    opts := fd.Options().(*descriptorpb.FieldOptions)
    if opts != nil && *opts.DebugRedact {
      switch fd.Kind() {
      case protoreflect.StringKind:
        m.Set(fd, protoreflect.ValueOfString(strings.Repeat("*",
        len(v.String()))))
      default:
        // TODO handle other types if needed
      }
    }
    return true
  })
}
```

We are done with the helper function. We can now move on to the business logic of the list command.

In ListContacts (pkg/addressbook/list.go), we will simply call the redactPrivateInfo on the messages that need to be checked and redacted. However, we will only do it if we receive a command line argument for redacting. Thus, we will receive a Boolean parameter in ListContacts to tell us whether to redact or not. The update ListContacts function looks like this:

```go
func ListContacts(db io.Reader, w io.Writer, redact bool) error {
  // data preparation
  for _, name := range names {
    contact := book.Contacts[name]

    if redact {
      switch c := contact.Kind.(type) {
      case *pb.Contact_Company:
        for _, email := range c.Company.Emails {
          redactPrivateInfo(email)
        }
        for _, phone := range c.Company.Phones {
          redactPrivateInfo(phone)
        }
      case *pb.Contact_Person:
```

```
      for _, phone := range c.Person.Phones {
        redactPrivateInfo(phone)
      }
      redactPrivateInfo(c.Person)
    }
  }

  // printing
  }
  return nil
}
```

The only thing left to do is add a command-line argument and pass the Boolean to this function. We will go to cmd/addressbook/addressbook.go, and update the Execute function like so:

```
func Execute() {
  // addCmd
  listCmd := flag.NewFlagSet("list", flag.ExitOnError)
  redact := listCmd.Bool("redact", false, "redacts private info")

  switch os.Args[1] {
  // add
  case "list":
    listCmd.Parse(os.Args[2:])
    listContacts(db, *redact)
  //default
  }
}
```

And we need to update the listContacts function in cmd/addressbook/list.go to receive and pass this Boolean to ListContacts. It looks like this:

```
func listContacts(db io.Reader, redact bool) {
  if err := addressbook.ListContacts(db, os.Stdout, redact); err !=
  nil {
    fmt.Printf("error: %s\n", err)
    os.Exit(1)
  }
}
```

That is it. We can now redact private information by simply passing a −redact flag to the addressbook. Let's remind ourselves of what we had before adding the -redact flag. If we execute the list command, we get this:

```
$ go run main.go list
name: Clément
last_updated: 03/11/2024 01:07:37
person: {
  email: "test@test.com"
  phones: {
    number: "11111111"
    type: TYPE_MOBILE
  }
}
```

With the new redact flag, we can now have the following:

```
$ go run main.go list -redact
name: Clément
last_updated: 03/11/2024 01:07:37
person: {
  email: "*************"
  phones: {
    number: "********"
    type: TYPE_MOBILE
  }
}
```

We have effectively hidden sensitive information in our data. We have just completed our AddressBook project. Congratulations!

Summary

In this chapter, we got more practical experience with Protobuf. We learned how to interact with Protobuf in Go. We touched upon as many Protobuf concepts as possible: maps, repeated, oneof, nested types, field options, and so on. Then, we learned how to serialize/deserialize data to/from a file. Finally, we linked everything to a CLI that has the add and list commands.

In the next chapter, we will create the same project in Python. The overall goal is to learn how to interact with Protobuf in this new language but also to show you that serialized data in Go can be read in Python and inversely.

Challenge

Here are a few challenges that might be fun:

- **Implement a search by name**. This should be pretty easy since we have a map of contacts.

- **Implement listing by starting letter**. The contact list is already sorted so it should not take too long.

- **Implement paging where only a subset of contact is returned at a time**. The design of this feature is not defined, just make sure that you can specify the number of contacts you want and that you get the first N contacts, then the next N, and so on.

8

Implementing the Address Book in Python

In the previous chapter, we created an address book in Golang. In this chapter, we are going to implement the same application in Python. The goal here is to, of course, learn about interacting with **Protocol Buffers** (**Protobuf**) in Python, but also to show you the interoperability of Protobuf binary. At the end of the chapter, we will have two applications that can serialize and deserialize our Address Book.

In this chapter we are going to cover the following main topics:

- Interacting with most Protobuf constructs in Python

- Writing/reading Protobuf encoded data to/from file

- Using Protobuf reflection to act on field data

By the end of the chapter, you will be able to interact with the Protobuf-generated code in Python. You will understand how to use the generated code in your application to serialize and deserialize any kind of data.

Technical requirements

All the code that you will see in this section can be found under the directory called chapter8 in the GitHub repository (https://github.com/PacktPublishing/Protocol-Buffers-Handbook).

> **Disclaimer**
> This chapter will focus on the Python implementation of the Address Book. This is in no way a Python tutorial. If you feel more comfortable with the Golang code, please revisit *Chapter 7* to check the implementation there.

The Address Book project

> **Disclaimer**
>
> If you read the section named *The project: Address Book* in *Chapter 7*, feel free to skip this section. It is here to make sure that, if you skipped the previous chapter, you could still get a sense of what the project is without flipping pages.

As mentioned in the introduction, this is a practical chapter. We are going to create a mini **command-line interface** (**CLI**) that lets us create and list contacts in an address book. Before we dive into the code, we will talk about the project itself and some of the architectural choices made in this project.

First, let us talk about the project. This address book project was heavily influenced by the official tutorial on the Protobuf documentation (`https://protobuf.dev/getting-started/pythontutorial/`). However, there are quite a few changes that I made to cover more Protobuf concepts. Here are the following changes that I made:

- Instead of adding only a person's contact in the address book, we will also be able to add a company's contact. This lets us use `oneof` because the contact will be either a company or a person.

- While the CLI will not cover searching the contact by name (this is a challenge for you), we made sure that it would be possible to do so. Instead of having a list of contacts, we have a `map` of strings to contact.

- For the sake of readability, we removed some of the extra fields that we did not need for this example to simplify the code a bit.

In other words, the goal of this project is to use as many concepts as possible provided by Protobuf in a simple but interesting project.

Now, as mentioned, this project is a CLI. It is going to have two commands. The `add` command will support the following flags:

- `name`: This is the contact's name.
- `kind`: This is either "cie", "company", "per", or "person". It tells us what kind of contact we are adding.
- `email`: This is the contact's email.
- `dep`: This is the contact's department. This is only used for company contact and is ignored otherwise. It can take the `hr` (human resources), or `cs` (customer service) value.
- `phone`: This is the contact's phone number.
- `type`: The type (for person) or department (for company) of phone number. It can take the home, `mobile`, or `work` value.

For example, we can add a person, with the `test@test.com` email address and the `11111111` mobile phone number, like so:

```
$ python main.py add --name "Clément" --kind "per" --phone "11111111"
--type "mobile" --email test@test.com
```

The `list` command will not support any flags just yet. However, once called, it will display contact information on the screen. For the previously added contact, we would get the following:

```
python main.py list
name: Clément
last_updated: 03/08/2024 07:24:55
person: {
  email: "test@test.com"
  phones: {
    number: "11111111"
    type: TYPE_MOBILE
  }
}
----------------------
```

You can see all the information that we are storing. On top of the data provided in flags, we also display the last updated time. This lets us use a well-known type called `Timestamp`.

Finally, all the information is stored in a file called `addressbook.db`. If it does not exist on the first `python main.py add`, it will be created and filled out.

Defining the schema

> **Disclaimer**
>
> Once again, this section is here for readers who skipped *Chapter 7*. The only difference is the code generation with `protoc`, which happens in the last few paragraphs, and the omission of the `go_package` option.

Starting a project involving Protobuf always starts by defining the schema. This is known as **schema-driven development (SDD)**. We essentially define the contract that needs to be fulfilled.

We are going to take a bottom-up approach to design this schema. We are going to start by defining what a `Person` contact looks like. As we saw in the description of the project, a person can have an email and multiple phone numbers. This looks like the following (`proto/addressbook.proto`):

```
message Person {
  //...
  string email = 1;
```

```
  repeated PhoneNumber phones = 2;
}
```

While the email is simply a string, the phone number will be represented by a nested message. This is because we want to be able to store the phone number and the type of phone number it is. As we know, the type of phone number can be mobile, work, or home. This means that we can represent this set of values with an enum. Knowing all of this, we now have the following:

```
message Person {
  message PhoneNumber {
    enum Type {
      TYPE_UNSPECIFIED = 0;
      TYPE_MOBILE = 1;
      TYPE_HOME = 2;
      TYPE_WORK = 3;
    }

    string number = 1;
    Type type = 2;
  }

  //email + phones
}
```

Hopefully, all of this should look very familiar now.

Now, let us go with the message for a Company contact. This will be similar to what we did with the Person message, however, in this case, we will have the possibility to add multiple phone numbers and emails with a respective company Department. This means that we are going to have two lists, one for storing the EmailAddress type and the other for storing the PhoneNumber type:

```
message Company {
  //...
  repeated EmailAddress emails = 1;
  repeated PhoneNumber phones = 2;
}
```

The EmailAddress type will contain the email address and Department related to that address:

```
message Company {
  message EmailAddress {
    string email = 1;
    Department department = 2;
  }
```

```
  //...
}
```

Similarly, the `PhoneNumber` type stores the number and its department:

```
message Company {
  message PhoneNumber {
    string number = 1;
    Department department = 2;
  }
  //...
}
```

Finally, `Department` will simply be an enum that lists all the departments available:

```
message Company {
  enum Department {
    DEPARTMENT_UNSPECIFIED = 0;
    DEPARTMENT_HR = 1;
    DEPARTMENT_CUSTOMER_SERVICE = 2;
  }
  //...
}
```

Next, we need to design `Contact`. As we know, a contact can be `Person` or `Company`. This means we can use `oneof` since we want to make sure that the data is mutually exclusive. Thus, we have the following:

```
message Contact {
  //...
  oneof kind {
    Person person = 2;
    Company company = 3;
  }
}
```

If you remember, we will also store the last updated time for the contact entry. For this, we will use the well-known `google.protobuf.Timestamp` type. This looks like the following:

```
import "google/protobuf/timestamp.proto";

message Contact {
  google.protobuf.Timestamp last_updated = 1;
  //...
}
```

Finally, we need to represent `AddressBook` itself. As mentioned, we want to be able to map a contact name to the contact entry. Thus, we will use a map of string (name) to `Contact`. The `AddressBook` is as simple as this:

```
message AddressBook {
   map<string, Contact> contacts = 1;
}
```

That is pretty much it for the schema. Let us make sure that we generate the code before continuing. We will use `--python_out`, which we saw in the chapter on Protobuf compiler (*Chapter 4*). We execute the following:

```
$ protoc --python_out=. proto/addressbook.proto
```

In the end, we should have the following files in the `proto` directory:

```
proto
├── addressbook_pb2.py
└── addressbook.proto
```

We just generated our code! We are now ready to move on and start tackling the main part of our application: the adding of entries. However, before we dive into that, we will need a few helper functions to read/write from/to files and convert a string (passed by the command line) into a `PhoneNumber` type or a `Company Department`.

Boilerplate code

Let us prepare some convenient helpers for the journey ahead. We know we will need to write/read to/from files and that we will need to transform some arguments, passed as strings, into Python types. Let us deal with the latter first since this is a very trivial task.

Converting strings to enum values

We are going to create two functions: `str_to_phone_type` and `str_to_department`. Both look similar since we are going to check the value of the string and derive an enum value out of it. Let us start with `str_to_phone_type`.

We know that the `PhoneType` enum contains the `TYPE_HOME`, `TYPE_MOBILE`, `TYPE_WORK`, and `TYPE_UNSPECIFIED` values. Thus, we will simply check for the `home`, `mobile`, and `work` values. If the string does not contain anything or a value outside of these, the phone type will be considered unspecified. The pseudocode for `str_to_phone_type` looks like the following:

```
def str_to_phone_type(s: str) Type:
   match s:
```

```
    case "home":
      return TYPE_HOME
    case "mobile":
      return TYPE_MOBILE
    case "work":
      return TYPE_WORK
    case _other:
      return TYPE_UNSPECIFIED
```

Now, to make this code viable, we should interact with the generated code. Unfortunately, reading the generated code in `proto/addressbook_pb2.py` is far from being intuitive. Instead, you can take a look at the following generated code documentation here: `https://protobuf.dev/reference/python/python-generated`. Under the *Nested Types* section, you will find the following explanation:

"*[if] Bar class is declared as a static member of Foo, you can refer to it as Foo.Bar.*"

In our case, this means that we will have access to the phone number type by writing `Person.PhoneNumber.Type` and we can access the values by prepending the name of the enum variant.

So, now that we know the name of the type, let us make the previous pseudocode correct. It looks like this (`main.py`):

```
import proto.addressbook_pb2 as pb


def str_to_phone_type(s: str) -> pb.Person.PhoneNumber.Type:
    match s:
        case "home":
            return pb.Person.PhoneNumber.Type.TYPE_HOME
        case "mobile":
            return pb.Person.PhoneNumber.Type.TYPE_MOBILE
        case "work":
            return pb.Person.PhoneNumber.Type.TYPE_WORK
        case _other:
            return pb.Person.PhoneNumber.Type.TYPE_UNSPECIFIED
```

Now, it is not hard to imagine what the `Department` type will look like. Since we know that `Department` is an enum inside the `Company` message, the type will be called `Company.Department`.

So, similar to `str_to_phone_type`, we can create a switch and derive the `Department` value from the string value:

```
def str_to_department(s: str) -> pb.Company.Department:
    match s:
        case "hr":
```

```
            return pb.Company.Department.DEPARTMENT_HR
        case "cs":
            return pb.Company.Department.DEPARTMENT_CUSTOMER_SERVICE
        case _other:
            return pb.Company.Department.DEPARTMENT_UNSPECIFIED
```

While this was a trivial task, this needed to be done, and during this process, we took our first look at the generated code types. We learned that the name of the generated type is given by the concatenation of the nested types' names, separated by a dot. Let us now focus on reading `AddressBook` from the database file.

Reading/writing from/to files

The application's core relies on the **input/output (I/O)** operations reading from the file and writing to the file. Each time we add a new contact, we will need to first read `AddressBook`, then add the contact to it, and finally, write `AddressBook` back to the file. Let us start with reading from the file.

First of all, we know that we will return `AddressBook`. Thus, we can simply write the following:

```
def read_from_db(...) -> pb.AddressBook:
    #...
```

Next, we need to think about how we are going to receive the file or file path as an argument. We could simply receive a string being the path of the file. We could also receive an opened file to simply read from it. While both are fine, I decided to go with a more generic approach: using `IO[bytes]`.

The main reason is that we are in the business logic of our application and thus we do not want to be tied to specific storage. By having this type of hint, we could easily reuse `read_from_db` with a different storage. For example, we could be reading from the network.

Thus, we now have the following:

```
from typing import IO

def read_from_db(db: IO[bytes]) -> pb.AddressBook:
    #...
```

Next, we are going to read the whole content from the reader into memory. For a small application like ours, this will be fine. We do not need to care about buffering and reading into chunks:

```
def read_from_db(db: IO[bytes]) -> pb.AddressBook:
    data = db.read()
    #...
```

Finally, now that we have the bytes out of the file, we can use a function provided by Protobuf for every message called `ParseFromString`. It takes some bytes and deserializes the data into a type. In our case, we will deserialize the bytes into `AddressBook`:

```
def read_from_db(db: IO[bytes]) -> pb.AddressBook:
    data = db.read()  book = pb.AddressBook()
    book.ParseFromString(data)
    return book
```

This is as simple as this; we created a function that takes bytes and turns them into a Protobuf-generated type.

The `write_to_db` function is similar to the `read_from_db` function. However, we will write the data to the database, and instead of using `ParseFromString`, we will use `SerializeToString`. The function looks like this:

```
def write_to_db(db: IO[bytes], book: pb.AddressBook):
    data = book.SerializeToString()
    db.write(data)
```

We now have all the boilerplate code needed to go ahead. We will now focus on adding entries to `AddressBook` and writing it to a file.

Adding entries

In this section, let us focus on adding a `Person` or a `Company` contact to `AddressBook`. We will start with the business logic and then we will link the business logic to the CLI part of our application.

The business logic

We will first write all the code related to the addition of contact. We will have two functions: `add_person` and `add_company`. Both functions are similar, however, they both receive different information as parameters. Let us first talk about the similarities between these two functions.

The first similarity is that both functions take `db` as a parameter. So, we have the following:

```
def add_person(db: IO[bytes], ...):
    #...

def add_company(db: IO[bytes], ...):
    #...
```

Next, both functions will use `read_from_db` to get the potentially already existing serialized data, and then `write_to_db` to save the newly updated data. Both functions will contain the following beginning and ending:

```
book = read_from_db(db)

if book.contacts is None:
  book.contacts = {}

#...
write_to_db(db, book)
```

Notice that we are initializing `book.Contacts` with a new dictionary. Since it can be `None` the first time, we create the db file there will be no `Contacts` data. Other than that, the code should be self-explanatory.

Now, let us get into the difference between the two `add` functions. These differences mostly come from the fact that we are dealing with two different types: `Person` and `Company`.

These two types are used in `oneof`. So, the most important thing that we need to be aware of is how `oneof` is used in Python. If you look at the *Oneof* section in the documentation (`https://protobuf.dev/reference/python/python-generated/#oneof`), you will read that the `oneof` fields are *"just like regular fields."* This means that if we have an existing contact, we can get the `person` instance by simply accessing the `Person` field. This is important to notice because this is not as easy in other languages.

Applying this, we now have the following:

```
def add_person(db: IO[bytes], ...):
  #...
  if name in book.contacts:
    person = book.contacts[name].person
  else:
    person = pb.Person()
  #...
```

Similarly, for `add_company`, it will look like this:

```
def add_company(db: IO[bytes], ...):
  #...
  if name in book.contacts:
    company = book.contacts[name].company
  else:
    company = pb.Company()
```

```
    #...
}
```

What is left is handling the data that we will get as parameters and adding it to AddressBook. As we know, for Person, we will need a name, an email, a phone number, and a phone type. As of now, we will consider that the name is never empty because we are going to check that later. However, we cannot assume that the email, phone number, and phone type are not empty. So, depending on whether the data exists, we are going to update Person or Company. For add_person, this will look like the following:

```
def add_person(db: IO[bytes], name: str, email: str, phone: str,
phone_type: str):
    #...
    if email is not None:
        person.email = email

    if phone is not None:
        nb = pb.Person.PhoneNumber()
        nb.number = phone
        nb.type = str_to_phone_type(phone_type)
        person.phones.append(nb)
    #...
```

For add_company, it will look similar to the Phone field in add_person, but we handle departments instead of types:

```
def add_company(db: IO[bytes], name: str, email: str, email_dep: str,
phone: str, phone_dep: str):
    #...
    if email is not None:
        addr = pb.Company.EmailAddress()
        addr.email = email
        addr.department = str_to_department(email_dep)
        company.emails.append(addr)

    if phone is not None:
        nb = pb.Company.PhoneNumber()
        nb.number = phone
        nb.department = str_to_department(phone_dep)
        company.phones.append(nb)
    #...
```

The main thing to note in these two code snippets is that we are appending to phones and emails. This is because we want to be able to add another phone number or email to an existing contact. If the contact already exists, we simply add the new information at the end of the Contact lists.

Finally, we simply need to create/recreate a `Contact` to override the information in `AddressBook.Contacts[name]`. While we could check once again whether the contact already exists and update accordingly, for the sake of brevity, we will simply create a new `Contact` every time. For `add_person`, we have the following:

```python
import google.protobuf.timestamp_pb2 as timestamppb

def add_person(db: IO[bytes], name: str, email: str, phone: str,
phone_type: str):
    #...
    contact = pb.Contact()
    update_ts = timestamppb.Timestamp()
    update_ts.GetCurrentTime()
    contact.last_updated.CopyFrom(update_ts)
    contact.person.CopyFrom(person)
    book.contacts[name].CopyFrom(contact)
    #...
```

For `add_company`, we have the following:

```python
def add_company(db: IO[bytes], name: str, email: str, email_dep: str,
phone: str, phone_dep: str):
    #...
    contact = pb.Contact()
    update_ts = timestamppb.Timestamp()
    update_ts.GetCurrentTime()
    contact.last_updated.CopyFrom(update_ts)
    contact.company.CopyFrom(company)
    book.contacts[name].CopyFrom(contact)
    #...
```

Notice the use of the function called `GetCurrentTime` in the `timestamppb` package. This is a function that creates a `Timestamp` from the current time. If you are familiar with the `datetime` package from Python's standard library and its now function, this is pretty much the same.

Finally, notice the use of the `CopyFrom` function. This copies a message into another. This is also the only way we can assign a complex value to a field. Before, when we were assigning strings, we could just use the normal assignment (a = b). For complex types (`Company`, `Timestamp`, etc.), we need to use `CopyFrom`.

Believe it or not, the business logic of adding contacts to `AddressBook` is finished. We created a way to take raw information (strings), create and update a contact, and serialize/deserialize data from db. We can now focus on integrating that with the CLI part of our application.

The CLI

> **Important note**
>
> The following section is here for the sake of completeness and is not related to using Protobuf in Python; it mostly binds the business logic to the CLI part of the application. Feel free to skip this part if you are not working on the AddressBook project.

Since we have the business logic for adding entries, the only thing left to do for the add command is to create the user interface. To do that, we are going to create the parsing and validation of command-line arguments. Let us start with the validation.

In our application, we need to make sure that a few things are consistent before passing them along to the business logic. For example, the name of the contact should never be empty since this is the main information we use to store the contact in the AddressBook.Contacts map.

Thankfully, Python has an amazing package to do CLI applications: argparse. With it, we will be able to specify all the flags, the restrictions for value, and the conditions it needs to fulfill before we are able to continue. We can create a parser with two subcommands like the following:

```python
if __name__ == '__main__':
    parser = argparse.ArgumentParser()
    subparsers = parser.add_subparsers(dest='command')

    add_parser = subparsers.add_parser('add')
    # add flags...

    list_parser = subparsers.add_parser('list')
    # list flags...
```

Notice that when we call the add_subparsers function, we pass the command value to the dest parameter. This will let us check the subcommand used by calling the command property on the value returned by the parsing. So, next, we will do the actual parsing of flags/commands and check whether the command is add or list:

```python
if __name__ == '__main__':
    #...
    args = parser.parse_args(sys.argv[1:])

    if args.command == "add":
        # add contact
    elif args.command == "list":
        # list contacts
    else:
        print("unknown command: ", args.command)
```

Now, before finishing with the specification of the flags, let us call the appropriate functions inside the `if` statements:

```python
if __name__ == '__main__':
    #...

    if args.command == "add":
        fd = os.open(DB_FILE_PATH, os.O_RDWR | os.O_CREAT)
        with os.fdopen(fd, 'rb+') as f:
            if args.kind in cie_keywords:
                add_company(f, args.name, args.email, args.dep, args.phone,
                args.type)
            elif args.kind in per_keywords:
                add_person(f, args.name, args.email, args.phone, args.type)
            else:
                print("error: unknown kind", args.kind)
    elif args.command == "list":
        # list contacts
    else:
        print("unknown command: ", args.command)
```

This code should be straightforward since this is just applying the function we wrote earlier, depending on the subcommand. However, notice that we open the database file with different permissions. For the add subcommand, we open with the read and write permission (O_RDWR), and the permission to create the file if it does not exist (O_CREAT). For add, we also specify that we are going to read binary. This is done by having the 'b' in "rb+" (r is for read and + is for adding writing permission).

The final thing to do is to add the flags to the subparsers. The list subparser will not have any just yet, so let us focus on the add one. Let us start with --name and --kind:

```python
add_parser = subparsers.add_parser('add')

add_parser.add_argument('--name',
                        required=True,
                        type=str,
                        help="the contact's name.")
add_parser.add_argument('--kind',
                        required=True,
                        type=str,
                        choices={"per", "person", "cie", "company"},
                        help="the kind of contact (company or
                        person).")
```

We defined the two flags with the restriction on the value being a string (type) and non-empty (required). On top of that, for `--kind`, we restrict the possible values (choices). Knowing this, the rest of the flags should be easy to understand:

```
add_parser.add_argument('--email',
                        type=str,
                        help="the contact's email.")
add_parser.add_argument('--dep',
                        type=str,
                        choices={"hr", "cs"},
                        help="the contact's department.")
add_parser.add_argument('--phone',
                        type=str,
                        help="the contact's phone number.")
add_parser.add_argument('--type',
                        type=str,
                        help="the type of phone number.")
```

This is it! We have our first command in the CLI. To try it, we can simply pass arguments at the end. For example, if we wanted to add `Person`, we would execute the following:

```
$ python main.py add --name "Clément" --kind "per" --phone "11111111"
--type "mobile" --email test@test.com
```

If we wanted to add a company, we would run the following:

```
$ python main.py add --name "Google" --kind "cie" --phone "11111111"
--type "hr" --email cs.test@test.com --dep "cs"
```

If you try to run these commands, you will notice that a file called `addressbook.db` has been created. This is where the data has been serialized. However, if you look at the data inside, you will see that it is binary. We need a better way to take a look at this data and this is why we need the `list` command.

Listing entries

Let us now focus on listing all the entries that are stored in the `addressbook.db` file. We will first start with the business logic and we will then go to the CLI part of the application.

The business logic

The job left for the CLI to be completed is rather small. We only need to read data from the database and display it on the standard output. Let us start by reading the data from the database:

```
def list_contacts(db: IO[bytes]):
  book = read_from_db(db)
  #...
```

Next, we can order the list of contacts alphabetically. This was mostly done for testing purposes, but it could be used for more advanced features such as filtering or paging. Here, we will simply focus on displaying all the contacts. The sorting looks like the following:

```
def list_contacts(db: IO[bytes]):
  book = read_from_db(db)
  for name in sorted(book.contacts.keys()):
    #...
```

Now that we have sorted names, we can just display the information:

```
def list_contacts(db: IO[bytes]):
  book = read_from_db(db)
  for name in sorted(book.contacts.keys()):
    contact = book.contacts[name]

    update_ts = contact.last_updated.ToDatetime()
    contact.ClearField("last_updated")
    print("name:", name)
    print("last_updated:", update_ts.strftime("%m/%d/%Y %H:%M:%S"))
    print(contact, end="")
    print("----------------------")
```

There are a few things to notice here. You can see that we are using the ToDateTime function on last_updated. If you remember, we used the timestamppb.GetCurrentTime() function to create a google.protobuf.Timestamp well-known type from a Python datetime. This is the opposite. We are taking Timestamp and turning it into datetime.

Finally, you can see that we are clearing (ClearField) last_updated. This is entirely for aesthetic reasons. Later in the code, we print the contact, which shows the Protobuf data in the Protobuf text format. We simply do not want the last_updated data to be displayed like this because it would show the internals of the Timestamp type. We simply want a beautiful date/time printed on the screen.

That is it for the business logic. Let us now switch to the CLI part of the feature.

The CLI

> **Important note**
> The following section is here for the sake of completeness and is not related to using Protobuf in Python; it is mostly for binding the business logic to the CLI part of the application. Feel free to skip this part if you are not working on the AddressBook project.

In this section, we will simply handle the command-line parsing. If you remember, in the main, we had something like the following:

```
if __name__ == '__main__':
    args = parser.parse_args(sys.argv[1:])

    if args.command == "add":
        # add contact
    elif args.command == "list":
        # list contacts
    else:
        print("unknown command: ", args.command)
```

We simply need to fill the list subcommand block with the following code:

```
with open(DB_FILE_PATH, 'rb') as f:
    list_contacts(f)
```

This time, you can see that we only need the read permission on the database, so we have rb, which stands for "read" and "binary."

Just like that, we now have the list subcommand in our CLI.

Let us try that by first adding some data to AddressBook:

```
$ python main.py add --name "Clément" --kind "per" --phone "11111111"
--type "mobile" --email test@test.com
```

Now, we can see the serialized data by running the following:

```
$ python main.py list
name: Clément
last_updated: 03/11/2024 01:07:37
person: {
  email: "test@test.com"
  phones: {
    number: "11111111"
    type: TYPE_MOBILE
```

```
    }
  }
```

As expected, we get the name, a formatted time, and all the information on the person.

Hiding sensitive data

The last thing that I want to add for this mini-project to be complete is to work with a field option. In our case, we will work with an option called `debug_redact`. This tells an application to redact the private information in the data. For us, this means hiding the phone numbers and email addresses.

Let us start by adding the option on the fields we want to redact in our `proto` file:

```
message Person {
  //...
  message PhoneNumber {
    string number = 1 [debug_redact = true];
    Type type = 2;
  }

  string email = 1 [debug_redact = true];
  repeated PhoneNumber phones = 2;
}

message Company {
  //...
  message EmailAddress {
    string email = 1 [debug_redact = true];
    Department department = 2;
  }

  message PhoneNumber {
    string number = 1 [debug_redact = true];
    Department department = 2;
  }
  //...
}
```

Next, as always, we need to compile the schema to generate the code out of it. We run the following command:

```
$ protoc --python_out=. proto/addressbook.proto
```

After that, we need a helper function to loop over the fields of a message, detect this option, and edit the information in the field. For this, we are going to use Protobuf reflection. We are going to create a function called `redact_private_info`, which looks like the following:

```
from google.protobuf.message import Message

def redact_private_info(msg: Message):
  #...
```

To use Protobuf reflection, we can access the DESCRIPTOR field of the message, which is of the Descriptor type (https://googleapis.dev/python/protobuf/latest/google/protobuf/descriptor.html#google.protobuf.descriptor.Descriptor). We can then simply loop over the fields:

```
def redact_private_info(msg: Message):
  for field in msg.DESCRIPTOR.fields:
    #...
```

From there, we can now check whether the current field has an option or not, and if yes, we can check if it has an option called `debug_redact`:

```
def redact_private_info(msg: Message):
  For field in msg.DESCRIPTOR.fields:
    if field.has_options:
      opts = field.GetOptions()

      if opts.debug_redact and field.type == descriptorpb.
      FieldDescriptorProto.TYPE_STRING:
        #...
```

Notice that we also checked that the current field type is string. This is because we only want to replace characters with an asterisk, however, you could specify other types. Check out the documentation here: https://googleapis.dev/python/protobuf/latest/google/protobuf/descriptor_pb2.html#google.protobuf.descriptor_pb2.FieldDescriptorProto.TYPE_BOOL.

Finally, let us replace the data of the strings with a series of asterisks. We will check whether the kind of data the field contains is a string and if that is the case, we will set the value to a string containing the same number of asterisks as the number of characters in the original string. We now have the following:

```
def redact_private_info(msg: Message):
  for field in msg.DESCRIPTOR.fields:
    if field.has_options:
      opts = field.GetOptions()
```

```
        if opts.debug_redact and field.type == descriptorpb.
FieldDescriptorProto.TYPE_STRING:
            old = getattr(msg, field.name)
            setattr(msg, field.name, '*' * len(old))
```

You can see that we use Python's getattr and setattr to get the old value of the message field called after the variable field.name value and set it to a string containing the len(old) asterisks.

We are done with the helper function. We can now move on to the business logic of the list command.

In list_contacts, we will simply call redact_private_info on the messages that need to be checked and redacted. However, we will only do it if we receive a command-line argument for redacting. Thus, we will receive a Boolean parameter in list_contacts to tell us whether to redact or not. The update list_contacts function looks like this:

```
def list_contacts(db: IO[bytes], redact: bool):
  book = read_from_db(db)
  for name in sorted(book.contacts.keys()):
    contact = book.contacts[name]

    if redact:
      if contact.WhichOneof("kind") == "person":
        redact_private_info(contact.person)
        for phone in contact.person.phones:
          redact_private_info(phone)
      elif contact.WhichOneof("kind") == "company":
        for phone in contact.company.phones:
          redact_private_info(phone)
        for email in contact.company.emails:
          redact_private_info(email)

    # printing
```

Other than the parameter that we added, what is important to notice is that we check which of the oneof fields was set with the function called WhichOneof. It returns the name of the field that has a value and thus we can simply compare it with the person and company strings.

The only thing left to do is add a command-line argument and pass the Boolean to this function. We will go to the main and add a flag for the list subparser. It looks like the following:

```
if __name__ == '__main__':
  #...
  list_parser = subparsers.add_parser('list')
  list_parser.add_argument(
    '--redact',
```

```
    nargs='?',
    const=True, default=False,
    type=bool,
    help='redacts private info'
  )
  #...
```

This argument is a little bit more complex than the other we wrote for the `add` subparser. Here, the `nargs` parameter tells the parser that we will have a 0 or 1 value for the `--redact` flag. This means that we can write `--redact` or `--redact=true`. The `const` parameter tells the parser the value the flag should have if it is in the form of `--redact`. Finally, the default value is `false`.

Finally, we need to pass this argument to the `list_contacts` function:

```
if __name__ == '__main__':
  #...
  elif args.command == "list":
    with open(DB_FILE_PATH, 'rb') as f:
      list_contacts(f, args.redact)
  #...
```

That is it. We can now redact private information by simply passing a `--redact` flag to `AddressBook`. Let us remind ourselves of what we had before adding the `--redact` flag. If we execute the list command, we get the following:

```
$ python main.py list
name: Clément
last_updated: 03/11/2024 01:07:37
person: {
  email: "test@test.com"
  phones: {
    number: "11111111"
    type: TYPE_MOBILE
  }
}
```

With the new `redact` flag, we can now have the following:

```
$ python main.py list --redact
name: Clément
last_updated: 03/11/2024 01:07:37
person: {
  email: "*************"
  phones: {
    number: "********"
```

```
    type: TYPE_MOBILE
  }
}
```

We effectively hid the sensitive information in our data. We just completed our `AddressBook` project. Congratulations!

Interoperability between Go and Python

The last thing that is important to note is that not only have we created the application in two languages, but we created two applications that can both understand the data serialized in `addressbook.db`.

Say we serialized data with the Go application, like the following:

```
$ cd chapter7
$ go run . add --kind per --name John --email john.doe@gmail.com
```

We can list all the elements of `chapter7/addressbook.db` with the Python CLI, like so:

```
$ cd chapter7
$ python ../chapter8/main.py list
name: John
last_updated: 03/26/2024 00:13:04
person {
  email: "john.doe@gmail.com"
}
---------------------
```

Inversely, we can serialize data in Python:

```
$ cd chapter8
$ python main.py add --kind per --name John --email john.doe@gmail.com
```

We can also list the elements with the Go CLI:

```
$ cd chapter7
$ go build -o addressbook
$ cd ../chapter8
$ ../chapter7/addressbook list
name: John
last_updated: 03/26/2024 00:16:34
person:  {
  email:  "john.doe@gmail.com"
```

```
}
```

This interoperability is due to the fact that Protobuf serializes data to binary and, until the deserialization parser understands that binary, we can have interoperability with any language. In other words, the serialized data is language agnostic.

Now, while we saw the benefits of having language-agnostic serialized data for this application (writing/reading to files), I encourage you to think about more use cases for such a feature. Additionally, if you do not know where to start, I recommend checking how gRPC transports its data across the wire.

Summary

In this chapter, we got more practical experience with Protobuf. We learned how to interact with Protobuf in Python and we touched upon as many Protobuf concepts as possible, including maps, repeated, oneofs, nested types, and field options. Then, we learned how to serialize/deserialize data to/from a file. Finally, we linked everything to a CLI, which has the `add` and `list` commands.

In the next chapter, we will create a `protoc` plugin in Go that lets us generate functions for data validation. With these functions, we will check whether the phone number and email address provided by the user are correct.

Challenge

Here are a few challenges that might be fun:

1. **Implement a search by name**. This should be pretty easy since we have a map of contacts.
2. **Implement listing by starting letter**. The contact list is already sorted so it should not take too long.
3. **Implement paging where only a subset of contact is returned at a time**. The design of this feature is not defined, so just make sure that you can specify the number of contacts you want and that you get the first N contacts, then the next N, and so on.

9
Developing a Protoc Plugin in Golang

In *Chapter 7*, we created an address book in Golang. In this chapter, we are going to iterate on the `AddressBook` and create a protoc plugin that generates Go code to validate the phone numbers and emails that the user inputs.

In this chapter, we are going to cover the following main topics:

- Defining Protobuf custom options
- Writing a custom protoc plugin

By the end of the chapter, you will be able to understand, at both theoretical and practical levels, what custom options and protoc plugins are. More importantly, you will be able to create them by yourself in Golang.

Technical requirements

All the code that you will see in this section can be found in the directory called `chapter9` in the GitHub repository (`https://github.com/PacktPublishing/Protocol-Buffers-Handbook`).

The project

In this chapter, we are going to create a protoc plugin that generates code validating the user input for a phone number and email address in our AddressBook application. This involves creating a Protobuf custom option and writing the actual plugin logic to generate the validation code.

The overall goal of this chapter is to have a CLI that checks the user input. Let's say the user enters the following command:

```
$ go run main.go add --kind per --name Clement --phone 111
```

It should return the following error:

```
error: 111 is not a valid phone number
```

Similarly, for emails, let's say the user enters the following:

```
$ go run main.go add --kind per --name Clement --email 111
```

It should return the following error:

```
error: 111 is not a valid email
```

And obviously, this should also work for company contacts.

On top of that, we will add an option to the protoc plugin that lets us choose which `regexp` rule to use in order to check the phone number. The default value will be a regexp used by Twilio to check E.164 (an international numbering plan).

So, if we tell the protoc plugin to use the `^abc$` regexp to check the phone number, only the phone number "abc" will be valid.

To attain the goal, we are going to first create a Protobuf custom option that will let us annotate a field to check. Then, we are going to write the plugin and generate code. And finally, we are going to integrate the generated code into our `AddressBook` application.

What are custom options?

Protobuf custom options are a way to annotate part of the schema with contextual information. Think of them as normal Protobuf options but with custom names. It is as simple as that. The reason they exist is also simple – it is extensibility. If you do not find the right option for your use case, just create one by yourself.

Now, let us face it, the first time we hear about Protobuf custom options, it is hard to understand why, except for the pretty abstract extensibility concept, we would need them. As such, I want to show you some examples of custom options and how they are used.

The first project that is very popular and uses Protobuf custom options is `protovalidate` (`https://github.com/bufbuild/protovalidate/`). If you have never heard of it, it is a "series of libraries designed to validate Protobuf messages at runtime based on user-defined validation rules".

Let us see an example. Let us say that we want the name of the user to never be empty. With protovalidate, we can just define our schema like so:

```
syntax = "proto3";

import "buf/validate/validate.proto";

message User {
    string name = 1 [(buf.validate.field).string.min_len = 1];
}
```

And after compiling the schema with the protovalidate protoc plugin, you can call a generated function that validates all the constraints you set on the field.

Obviously, there is way more to protovalidate, and I invite you to check out the project and the supported languages (https://github.com/bufbuild#protovalidate). As you can probably guess, protovalidate is the inspiration for this chapter, and it is the most practical use of custom options that I have seen.

Another project worth mentioning is gRPC-Gateway (https://github.com/grpc-ecosystem/grpc-gateway). While gRPC is out of the scope of this book, it is important that, by default, gRPC uses Protobuf to transport data across a network. However, since a lot of frontend developers are used to JSON due to its great interaction with JavaScript and are not ready/able to change, gRPC-Gateway generates a reverse proxy that provides a way for the frontend to send JSON, translate it to Protobuf, and send the Protobuf data to the backend.

Let's see an example. Let's say that we have a web API getting a message as a parameter and returning the same message as a response, like the echo command in Unix. We could define the following schema:

```
syntax = "proto3";

message StringMessage {
    string value = 1;
}

service YourService {
    rpc Echo(StringMessage) returns (StringMessage) {
        option (google.api.http) = {
            post: "/v1/example/echo"
            body: "*"
        };
    }
}
```

The option here lets the gRPC-Gateway protoc plugin generate traditional REST API endpoints. In this case, it will create a `POST` endpoint, accessible through the `"/v1/example/echo"` route and accepting anything as body.

Once we are ready, we can send to `$URL/v1/example/echo` a JSON as follows:

```
{
    value: "hello world"
}
```

Then, the generated code will transform that JSON into a StringMessage, and you will receive that Protobuf message in your backend. Assuming that the backend returns a StringMessage with a value equal to `"hello world"`, the generated code will transform the Protobuf data back to JSON, and the frontend will receive JSON.

Once again, there is way more to the project than what I am describing here. I invite you to check out the project and try it out by yourself.

Now that we know what custom options are and what they are used for, we can start defining our own.

A custom option

Before starting to define the actual option, we need to understand what it will look like. This will guide us in choosing the right kind of option. For this project, we will keep it simple and define an option that will let us write this kind of message:

```
message Person {
  option (validate.field) = {
    name: "email",
    type: TYPE_EMAIL,
  };
  //...
  string email = 1 [debug_redact = true];
}
```

In other words, we have an option called `field` in the `validate` package that can be used in a message and contains the `name` and `type` fields. The `name` field defines the name of the field to check. In this case, this is an email in the `Person` message. The `type` field tells the plugin which function to generate (email or phone validation) for this field.

Now, to define such an option, we need to extend a message provided with Protobuf (in `descriptor.proto`) `google.protobuf.MessageOptions`. I encourage you to look at all the other options that you can create, but if you look specifically at `MessageOptions`, you will see the following line:

```
message MessageOptions {
  //...
  // Clients can define custom options in extensions of this message.
  extensions 1000 to max;
}
```

This line tells us the range of field tags that are available for custom options. In this case, if we define a custom option to be used in `MessageOptions`, this option can only have a field with a tag between 1,000 and 536,870,911 (the maximum value for a tag).

On top of the range given by the extensions statement, Protobuf has a global registry for known extensions (`https://github.com/protocolbuffers/protobuf/blob/main/docs/options.md`). It records the field tags already used by other custom options. As we saw in *Chapter 6*, reusing a tag can lead to undefined behaviors. Thus, this registry records all the information needed so that people do not reuse already existing tags.

At the time of the writing, the last tag number used is `1187`. As such, we will use the tag `1188`. So, we define the following schema (`proto/validate/custom_options.proto`):

```
syntax = "proto3";

package validate;

import "google/protobuf/descriptor.proto";

option go_package = "github.com/PacktPublishing/Protocol-Buffers-
Handbook/chapter9/proto/validate";

extend google.protobuf.MessageOptions {
  FieldConstraints field = 1188;
}

message FieldConstraints {
  enum Type {
    TYPE_UNSPECIFIED = 0;
    TYPE_EMAIL = 1;
    TYPE_PHONE = 2;
  }
```

```
    string name = 1;
    Type type = 2;
}
```

At this point in this book, everything should be very familiar. The main thing that we did not go into detail previously is the extend part. Here, we extend the message called MessageOptions in the google.protobuf package, and as we saw, we define a field with the tag 1188.

Note that here we are defining a "complex" option (with the type not being scalar such as bool, ...), but you could have a simpler option that looks like the following:

```
extend google.protobuf.MessageOptions {
    bool is_awesome = 1188;
}
```

And then, you could provide a simple true or false value for it.

The last thing to do is generate Go code from this custom option. This will let us use reflection in the plugin when we deal with getting information from the schema. This is very similar to what we have done so far:

```
$ protoc --go_out=. --go_opt=paths=source_relative proto/validate/
custom_options.proto
```

You should now have a custom_options.pb.go file inside the proto/validate directory. We are done with the custom option. We can now start to think about the protoc plugin.

What are protoc plugins?

Once again, before diving into the actual code of the plugin, let us try to understand what protoc plugins are and what they do.

As we saw in the section on custom options, protoc plugins and custom options are generally used together. The custom options provide contextual information, and the plugin gets that information and acts on it. This action, more often than not, is a generation of some sort of code. We have already discussed protovalidate and gRPC-Gateway generating some code that can be used in your business logic.

Even though, in this section, we are going to generate code, it is important to understand that protoc plugins can do other things than generate code.

You can also, for example, generate documentation following the OpenAPI specification with the protoc-gen-openapiv2 provided by gRPC-Gateway. Let's say you have the following schema:

```
syntax = "proto3";

import "google/api/annotations.proto";
import "protoc-gen-openapiv2/options/annotations.proto";

option (grpc.gateway.protoc_gen_openapiv2.options.openapiv2_swagger) =
{
  info: {
    title: "Echo API";
    version: "1.0";
    contact: {
      name: "Clement Jean";
      email: "myemail@gmail.com";
    };
    license: {
      name: "BSD 3-Clause License";
    };
  };

  schemes: HTTPS;
  consumes: "application/json";
  produces: "application/json";
};

message EchoRequest {
  string name = 1;
}

message EchoResponse {
  string greeting = 1;
}

service EchoService {
  rpc Echo(EchoRequest) returns (EchoResponse) {
    option (google.api.http) = {
      get: "/api/v1/echo"
    };
  };
}
```

You can generate the documentation presented in *Figure 9.1*. This is especially useful for large and/or user-facing projects. This provides your user with proper documentation and a way to interact with your API directly from inside it (see the **Try it out** button).

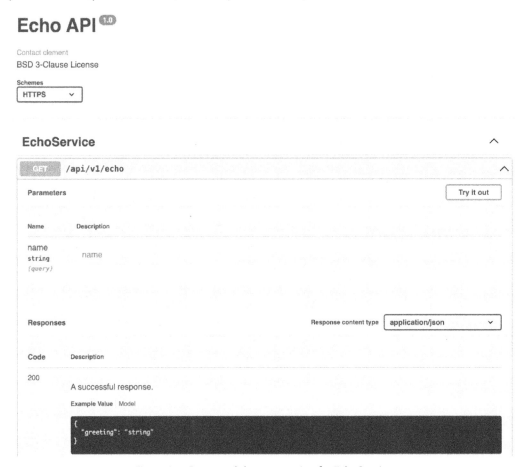

Figure 9.1: Generated documentation for EchoService

Other than generating code or documentation, you could also generate some kind of graph from your proto files. As we know, Protobuf describes its concepts in terms of descriptors. We could walk through all these descriptors and generate GraphViz code (`https://graphviz.org/`). See *Figure 9.2* for an example.

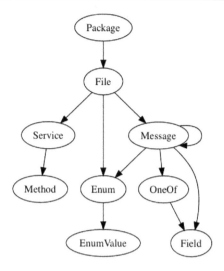

Figure 9.2: A graph of the Protobuf schema AST (source: https://github.com/lyft/protoc-gen-star)

Now that we know what a protoc plugin is and what we can do with one, let's build our own.

The plugin

> **Important message**
>
> This section will use Golang. If you are not confident about using Golang, I would still encourage you to try and get a sense of what is going on. The best alternative to write such a plugin is C++, although it is a less beginner-friendly language.

Let us start creating our own protoc plugin. Since the protogen API (`https://pkg.go.dev/google.golang.org/protobuf/compiler/protogen`) is easy to use, we are going to build it in Golang. Similarly to the work we did in *Chapter 7*, we are going to separate the business logic (`pkg`) and the CLI (`cmd`) part of our application. So, we will have the following file structure:

```
.
├── cmd
│   └── protoc-gen-check
│       └── ...
├── go.mod
├── pkg
│   └── protoc-gen-check
│       └── ...
└── proto
    └── validate
```

```
├── custom_options.pb.go
└── custom_options.proto
```

Note that we are calling our protoc plugin `protoc-gen-check`. This is a conventional name. If you use the `--custom_out` flag in the `protoc` command, since this is not an original flag, it will search for a binary called `protoc-gen-custom` in your PATH. Here, we call our folder `protoc-gen-check` so that, later on, we can just run `go build` on `cmd/protoc-gen-check` and the binary will have the name of the directory.

Now that we know that, let us start with the `pkg` part of our application.

Getting all the messages

As we know, we have a custom option that extends `MessageOptions`. This means that our plugin will only target messages, and we can skip all the rest. As such, we are going to need a function that gets all the `protogen.Message` (https://pkg.go.dev/google.golang.org/protobuf/compiler/protogen#Message) from `protogen.File` (https://pkg.go.dev/google.golang.org/protobuf/compiler/protogen#File).

In `pkg/protoc-gen-check/message.go`, we will create an exported function called `GetAllMessages` that goes through the messages in a file, adds them to the slice, and calls the recursive function, `getAllNestedMessages`. Here is what this looks like:

```go
package protoc_gen_check

import "google.golang.org/protobuf/compiler/protogen"

func GetAllMessages(file *protogen.File) (res []*protogen.Message) {
  for _, msg := range file.Messages {
    res = append(res, msg)
    res = append(res, getAllNestedMessages(msg)...)
  }
  return res
}
```

As we know, messages can be nested in Protobuf. As such, `getAllNestedMessages` is a function that recursively enters all the nested messages in a given message. It will also return a list of messages. Here is the definition of `getAllNestedMessages`:

```go
func getAllNestedMessages(msg *protogen.Message) (res []*protogen.Message) {
  for _, nested := range msg.Messages {
    if !nested.Desc.IsMapEntry() {
      res = append(res, nested)
    }
```

```
    res = append(res, getAllNestedMessages(nested)...)
  }
  return res
}
```

The most important thing to note is that we are only adding a message to the list if this is not a map entry. If you recall, a map in Protobuf is just syntax sugar around a repeated MapEntry (see *Chapter 3*). These messages are not valuable to us; we only care about "real" types, not the ones generated by the compiler.

That is all for the boilerplate; we can now move on to the meat of the application – the CLI.

Defining a Protoc plugin

Writing a simple protoc plugin is surprisingly easy. If you look at the documentation of protogen. Options (https://pkg.go.dev/google.golang.org/protobuf/compiler/protogen#Options), you can see that we need to define some plugin option object, and we can now call the Run function on it. This function takes a lambda function as param with protogen. Plugin (https://pkg.go.dev/google.golang.org/protobuf/compiler/protogen#Plugin) as a parameter. This Plugin object is the root object and contains a list of files being compiled. So, for now, we can define the following main function (cmd/protoc-gen-check):

```
import (
  "google.golang.org/protobuf/compiler/protogen"
)

func main() {
  opts := protogen.Options{}

  opts.Run(func(plugin *protogen.Plugin) error {
    for _, f := range plugin.Files {
      if !f.Generate {
        continue
      }
      // TODO: generate code
    }
    return nil
  })
}
```

Note the check for the `Generate` field. It tells you whether you need to generate code for a given file or not. This is not too intuitive at first, but if you look at all the files in the `protogen.Plugin`, you will see that all the files included in the proto file are present. In our case, we will have the following:

- `google/protobuf/timestamp.proto`
- `google/protobuf/descriptor.proto`
- `validate/custom_options.proto`

And we do not want to check these unnecessarily. We are sure they do not have our custom Protobuf option.

The next thing to do is create the actual file in which we are going to write the generated code. This looks like the following:

```go
const (
  extension  = "check.pb.go"
  pluginName = "protoc-gen-check"
)

func main() {
  //..

  opts.Run(func(plugin *protogen.Plugin) error {
    for _, f := range plugin.Files {
      //...
      generateFile(plugin, f)
    }
    return nil
  })
}

func generateFile(plugin *protogen.Plugin, file *protogen.File) {
  filename := file.GeneratedFilenamePrefix + "_" + extension
  gen := plugin.NewGeneratedFile(filename, file.GoImportPath)
  //...
}
```

The most important thing to note here is that we are constructing a filename with `GeneratedFilenamePrefix` and `extension`, and we create the file at `GoImportPath`. `GeneratedFilenamePrefix` is basically the name of the file we compile without the `.proto` extension. So, if we have `proto/test.proto`, it will be `test`. We concatenate an underscore and our own extension (`check.pb.go`) to that.

`GoImportPath` contains the value that we set to `go_package` in our proto file. This tells protoc the path, from the root of the project, where the file should be created.

Now that we have our generated file, we can start writing to it. We do that with the `P()` member function. It takes variadic arguments to write and prints them in a line. So, we will write the following to our file:

```
func generateFile(plugin *protogen.Plugin, file *protogen.File) {
  //...
  gen.P("// Code generated by ", pluginName, ". DO NOT EDIT.")
  gen.P()
  gen.P("package ", file.GoPackageName)
  //...
}
```

The first line is a conventional comment at the beginning of every generated code file. It warns the reader that this code was generated and should not be edited manually. The next non-empty line is the Go package statement. We use the `GoPackageName` field, which is the name of the package the generated code should be in. This should be the last part of `GoImportPath` that we saw previously.

Next, we need to generate the `isEmail` and `isPhoneNumber` functions that will check the validity of their input. We will create a function called `generatFunctions` and start writing these functions in the generated File. It looks like so:

```
func generateFile(plugin *protogen.Plugin, file *protogen.File,
phoneRegexp *string) {
  //...

  gen.P()
  gen.P("import \"net/mail\"")
  gen.P("import \"regexp\"")
  gen.P("import \"strings\"")
  gen.P()
  gen.P("var phoneRegexp = regexp.MustCompile(`^\\+[1-9]\\d{1,14}$`)")

  generateFunctions(gen, file)
}

func generateFunctions(gen *protogen.GeneratedFile, file *protogen.
File) {
  gen.P(`func isEmail(s string) bool {
    _, err := mail.ParseAddress(s)
    return err == nil
  }`)
  gen.P()
  gen.P(`func isPhoneNumber(s string) bool {
    s = strings.ReplaceAll(s, " ", "")
    return phoneRegexp.Find([]byte(s)) != nil
```

```
  }`)
  //...
}
```

Note that we added some imports and a global variable in the generateFile function. These are used in the two generated functions.

Then, we can generate the member function for the messages containing our custom option. To check whether a message contains a custom option and get its value, we can use the proto. GetExtension function (https://pkg.go.dev/google.golang.org/protobuf/proto#GetExtension). So, we can write the following:

```
import (
  //...
  pkg "github.com/PacktPublishing/Protocol-Buffers-Handbook/chapter9/
  pkg/protoc-gen-check"
  "github.com/PacktPublishing/Protocol-Buffers-Handbook/chapter9/
  proto/validate"
)
func generateFunctions(gen *protogen.GeneratedFile, file *protogen.
File) {
  //...
  gen.P()

  for _, msg := range pkg.GetAllMessages(file) {
    opts := msg.Desc.Options()
    value, _ := proto.GetExtension(opts, validate.E_Field).(*validate.
    FieldConstraints)

    if value == nil {
      continue
    }
    //...
}
```

Note the use of the generated variable called E_Field. This was generated when we compiled our validate.proto file and says that we have an extension field called field. Here, we try to get this extension in every message we find, and we cast its value into FieldConstraints (the message we defined in proto/validate/validate.proto). If the value is nil, it means that the current message does not have our custom option, so we can just skip it.

The next step is to generate the functions. We can do it like so:

```
import (
  //...
```

```go
    "fmt"
    "slices"

    "google.golang.org/protobuf/reflect/protoreflect"
)

func generateFunctions(gen *protogen.GeneratedFile, file *protogen.
File) {
  //...
  for _, msg := range pkg.GetAllMessages(file) {
    //...

    fieldDesc := msg.Desc.Fields().ByName(protoreflect.Name(value.
    Name))
    if fieldDesc == nil {
      continue
    }
    fieldIdx := slices.IndexFunc(msg.Fields, func(f *protogen.Field)
    bool {
      return f.Desc == fieldDesc
    })
    fieldName := fmt.Sprintf("x.%s", msg.Fields[fieldIdx].GoName)

    switch value.Type {
    case validate.FieldConstraints_TYPE_PHONE:
      gen.P("func (x ", msg.GoIdent, ") CheckPhone() error {")
      gen.P("if !isPhoneNumber(", fieldName, ") { return fmt.
      Errorf(\"%s is not a valid phone number\", ", fieldName, ") }")
      gen.P("return nil")
      gen.P("}")
      gen.P()
    case validate.FieldConstraints_TYPE_EMAIL:
      gen.P("func (x ", msg.GoIdent, ") CheckEmail() error {")
      gen.P("if !isEmail(", fieldName, ") { return fmt.Errorf(\"%s is
      not a valid email\", ", fieldName, ") }")
      gen.P("return nil")
      gen.P("}")
      gen.P()
    }
  }
}
```

While this code looks a little bit intimidating, this is simple. We first look for the field with the name provided in the `FieldConstraints.Name`. If we do not find it, we skip the option; otherwise, we get its name and create the following `fieldName – x.${NAME}`. The x value will be the name of the receiver parameter. And if you look at the switch cases, you will see the following:

```
gen.P("func (x ", msg.GoIdent, ...)
```

That is our receiver parameter.

After that, we simply create a function depending on the `FieldConstraints.Type`. If we have `TYPE_PHONE`, we create the following (for `Person_PhoneNumber`):

```
func (x Person_PhoneNumber) CheckPhone() error {
  if !isPhoneNumber(x.Number) {
    return fmt.Errorf("%s is not a valid phone number", x.Number)
  }
  return nil
}
```

And if we have `TYPE_EMAIL`, we create the following (for `Person`):

```
func (x Person) CheckEmail() error {
  if !isEmail(x.Email) {
    return fmt.Errorf("%s is not a valid email", x.Email)
  }
  return nil
}
```

That's it! We have created a basic plugin that can generate functions for messages containing our custom option. We can now build it by running the following command:

```
$ go build ./cmd/protoc-gen-check
```

However, for the newly created binary to be useful, we still need to have a schema containing our custom option. We are now going to use the `AddressBook` project that we created in *Chapter 7* and update it to have input validation for email and phone numbers.

Updating the AddressBook

As we are going to work with the application we wrote in *Chapter 7*, let's copy it over to the `chapter9` directory:

```
$ cp -R ../chapter7/cmd/addressbook cmd
$ cp -R ../chapter7/pkg/addressbook pkg
$ cp ../chapter7/main.go .
$ cp ../chapter7/proto/addressbook.proto proto
```

Now, because we were using a Go module name including `chapter7`, we will need to replace all the occurrences by `chapter9`. On Linux/Mac, we can run the following command:

```
$ find . -type f -exec sh -c "sed -i '' -e 's/chapter7/chapter9/g' {}" ";"
```

And on Windows (Powershell), we can run the following:

```
$ Get-ChildItem -Recurse -File -Include *.proto,*.go,go.mod | ForEach { (Get-Content $_ | ForEach { $_ -replace 'chapter7', 'chapter9' }) | Set-Content $_ }
```

We are now all set up to start.

The first step is to update our proto file to use our custom option. To do that, we will import our `validate.proto` file and start adding options with their respective values. Here is the newly updated `proto/addressbook.proto` file:

```
syntax = "proto3";

import "google/protobuf/timestamp.proto";
import "validate/custom_options.proto";

option go_package = "github.com/PacktPublishing/Protocol-Buffers-Handbook/chapter9/proto";
message Person {
  option (validate.field) = {
    name: "email",
    type: TYPE_EMAIL,
  };

  message PhoneNumber {
    option (validate.field) = {
      name: "number",
      type: TYPE_PHONE,
    };
    //...
    string number = 1 [debug_redact = true];
  }

  //...
  string email = 1 [debug_redact = true];
}

message Company {
  //...
```

```
message EmailAddress {
  option (validate.field) = {
    name: "email",
    type: TYPE_EMAIL,
  };

  //...
  string email = 1 [debug_redact = true];
}

message PhoneNumber {
  option (validate.field) = {
    name: "number",
    type: TYPE_PHONE,
  };

  //...
  string number = 1 [debug_redact = true];
}
//...
}

//...
```

As you can see, we basically target all the number and email fields.

Now that we have that, we can generate the code out of this schema thanks to our custom plugin. To do this, we are going to use the --plugin flag provided by protoc. It lets us specify where the binary is for a given plugin. So, we can first build our protoc plugin, get a binary, and then tell protoc the name of the plugin and its location. It looks like this:

```
$ go build cmd/protoc-gen-check
$ protoc --plugin=protoc-gen-check=protoc-gen-check -Iproto --go_
out=proto --go_opt=paths=source_relative --check_out=proto --check_
opt=paths=source_relative proto/addressbook.proto
```

You should now have both addressbook.pb.go and addressbook_check.pb.go in your proto directory.

Also, note that we are providing an option (called paths) to our plugin. However, we did not define any in our code. This is because protoc provides by default a few options to every plugin. If you are interested in finding more, search for paths at https://github.com/protocolbuffers/protobuf-go/blob/master/compiler/protogen/protogen.go.

If you now open `addressbook_check.pb.go`, you should see some functions like the following:

```
func (x Company_EmailAddress) CheckEmail() error {
  if !isEmail(x.Email) {
    return fmt.Errorf("%s is not a valid email", x.Email)
  }
  return nil
}
```

Also, note that we did not generate code for messages not containing the custom option (`Contact` and `AddressBook`).

We can update our `AddressBook` business logic to use these generated functions and return an error if an email address or a phone number is incorrect. We will go into `pkg/addressbook` and change the `AddPerson` and `AddCompany` functions in `add.go`. For `AddPerson`, this will look like the following:

```
func AddPerson(db io.ReadWriter, name, email, phoneNb, phoneType
string) error {
  //...
  if len(email) != 0 {
    person.Email = email

    if err := person.CheckEmail(); err != nil {
      return err
    }
  }

  if len(phoneNb) != 0 {
    nb := ...
    if err := nb.CheckPhone(); err != nil {
      return err
    }

    person.Phones = append(person.Phones, nb)
  }
  //...
}
```

For the sake of brevity, I will let you do, by yourself, a similar thing for `AddCompany`.

Once this is done, we are ready to experiment with our validation. We will run our `AddressBook` application with correct and wrong phone numbers/emails. For example, a correct phone number could be the following:

```
$ go run main.go add --kind per --name Clement --phone +14155552671
```

We should not have an error after running that. However, let's say we run the following:

```
$ go run main.go add --kind per --name Clement --phone abc
```

We should get the following message:

```
error: abc is not a valid phone number
```

Similarly, for emails, the following should not return errors:

```
$ go run main.go add --kind per --name Clement --email my.email@gmail.
com
```

However, let's say we run the following:

```
$ go run main.go add --kind per --name Clement --email 123
```

That should return the following error:

```
error: 123 is not a valid email
```

Everything works as expected. You can try the same commands on a company contact. You should have the same errors.

As you know, we use Twilio regex to check phone numbers. Would it not be cool if we could pass a custom regex as a parameter of our plugin to check more specific phone numbers?

Adding a protoc plugin option

You might already have an idea of how to add options to the plugin. If you remember, we created an instance of `protogen.Options` in our main plugin. This `Options` object can work with the `flags` package in the standard library. We simply need to define our flags and pass the `Set` function to the `Options` instance. This looks like this (`cmd/protoc-gen-check/main.go`):

```
import (
  "flags"
  //...
)

func main() {
  var flags flag.FlagSet
```

```
    phoneRegexp := flags.String("phone_regexp", "", "custom regex for
    phone checking.")
    opts := protogen.Options{
      ParamFunc: flags.Set,
    }
    //...
  }
```

If you are not familiar with the flags package from the standard library, we define a flag of type `string`, the name `phone_regexp`, and the default value of the empty string.

We can now pass the `phoneRegexp` variable to our `generateFile` function, and depending on whether this value is set or not, we will define a different `phoneRegexp` variable in our generated code. We have the following:

```
func main() {
  //...
  opts.Run(func(plugin *protogen.Plugin) error {
    for _, f := range plugin.Files {
      //....
      generateFile(plugin, f, phoneRegexp)
    }
    return nil
  })
}

func generateFile(plugin *protogen.Plugin, file *protogen.File,
phoneRegexp *string) {
  //...
  if len(*phoneRegexp) == 0 {
    gen.P("var phoneRegexp = regexp.MustCompile(`^\\+[1-
    9]\\d{1,14}$`)")
  } else {
    gen.P("var phoneRegexp = regexp.MustCompile(`", *phoneRegexp,
    "`)")
  }
  //...
}
```

It is as simple as that. We can then recompile our plugin:

```
$ go build cmd/protoc-gen-check
```

Then, we regenerate our code with a different regexp:

> **Note**
>
> "Due to some parsing logic in the protobuf compiler, adding a regex containing a comma will result in a parsing error. This is unfortunate but the goal of this section was mostly about showing how to add an option to your protoc plugin."

```
$ protoc --plugin=protoc-gen-check=protoc-gen-check -Iproto --go_
out=proto --go_opt=paths=source_relative --check_out=proto --check_
opt=paths=source_relative,phone_regexp='^abc$' proto/addressbook.proto
```

You should now be able to see the following line in `proto/addressbook_check.pb.go`:

```
var phoneRegexp = regexp.MustCompile(`^abc$`)
```

This means that if we now provide a phone number that is different from `abc`, it will be invalid. Let's say we run the following:

```
$ go run main.go add --kind per --name Clement --phone abc
```

We should not have any error. However, let's say we run the following:

```
$ go run main.go add --kind per --name Clement --phone +14155552671
```

We should get the following error:

```
error: +14155552671 is not a valid phone number
```

This also works as expected. Obviously, you should probably not use `abc` as a valid phone number, but I chose this dull value to make it clear that we are using a regexp that is different from the one we used before.

That's it! We have made a configurable plugin. Be proud of yourself because this is not a small feat.

Summary

In this chapter, we looked at what Protobuf custom options and protoc plugins are. We saw that they work in pairs to achieve some kind of generation (code, documentation, etc.). We then saw how to develop a plugin in Golang and how to make it configurable. Finally, we applied our knowledge of the `AddressBook` project to validate user input.

In the next chapter, we will go over the different ways to build projects that use Protobuf. We will talk about how to build a project manually, with Buf and Bazel.

Challenges

- Implement the same plugin that generates Python code and updates the Python AddressBook

- Implement a plugin (`protoc-gen-redact`) that generates a Redact function, implementing the redaction of data labeled with the `debug_redact` field option

- Add a protoc plugin option to choose the character that should be used for redacting (the default is `*`)

10
Advanced Build

In *Chapter 4*, we talked about the **Protobuf compiler** (**protoc**). While this is the way in which we built our proto files up until now to learn about Protobuf, there are other build tools that are widely used in the industry, and it is important to be aware of them. In this chapter, we are going to cover two other ways to build Protobuf projects. We are first going to recapitulate what we have learned about protoc, and then we will see how to use Buf and Bazel.

In this chapter, we are going to cover the following main topics:

- Building with Makefile
- Building with Buf
- Building with Bazel

By the end of the chapter, you will be able to understand, at both theoretical and practical levels, what custom options and the protoc plugins are. More importantly, you will be able to create them by yourself in Golang.

Technical requirements

All the code that you will see in this section can be found in the directory called `chapter10` in the GitHub repository (`https://github.com/PacktPublishing/Protocol-Buffers-Handbook`).

The sample project

In this chapter, in order to not wrestle too much with the build system, we are going to use a smaller Go project than the AddressBook. This project, however, is designed to represent the minimal project in which a build system is valuable. From there, you should be able to, with a bit more configuration, adapt the builds we create here to your own project.

The sample project will have the following file structure:

```
.
├─ go.mod
├─ go.sum
├─ main.go
└─ proto
    ├─ test.proto
    └─ v1
        └─ test.proto
```

Notice that we are nesting proto files in the `proto` directory and the rest of the application is in the root directory. We decided to nest the proto files by at least one level because in this chapter we want to show how to discover multiple proto files that are stored in multiple levels of the `proto` directory.

> **Important message**
>
> We will copy this sample project three times. We will have it in the `makefile`, `buf`, and `bazel` directories (see `chapter10` in the GitHub repository). In the following code, we will assume that we are in the `makefile` directory. This means that our Go module will be named `github.com/PacktPublishing/Protocol-Buffers-Handbook/chapter10/makefile`. However, in the `buf` and `bazel` directories, the Go module will be named `github.com/PacktPublishing/Protocol-Buffers-Handbook/chapter10/buf` and `github.com/PacktPublishing/Protocol-Buffers-Handbook/chapter10/bazel` respectively.

Next, both `test.proto` files will be very similar. The only thing we care about here is whether the code was generated or not. The `proto/test.proto` file will look like the following:

```
syntax = "proto3";

option go_package = "github.com/PacktPublishing/Protocol-Buffers-Handbook/chapter10/makefile/proto";

message Test {
   string name = 1;
}
```

And the `proto/v1/test.proto` file will look like this:

```
syntax = "proto3";

option go_package = "github.com/PacktPublishing/Protocol-Buffers-Handbook/chapter10/makefile/proto/v1";
```

```
message Test {
   string name = 1;
}
```

The main difference is the go_package into which the code will be generated.

Next, the Go application is very simple. It will print two Test instances, one from proto/test.proto and the other from proto/v1/test.proto. And more precisely, it will print them in the Protobuf Text format. As such, the main.go file will look like the following:

```
package main

import (
   "fmt"

   "google.golang.org/protobuf/encoding/prototext"

   pb "github.com/PacktPublishing/Protocol-Buffers-Handbook/chapter10/
   makefile/proto"
   pbV1 "github.com/PacktPublishing/Protocol-Buffers-Handbook/
   chapter10/makefile/proto/v1"
)

func main() {
   fmt.Println(prototext.Format(&pb.Test{Name: "my name"}))
   fmt.Println(prototext.Format(&pbV1.Test{Name: "my name v1"}))
}
```

Finally, the go.mod file will contain the dependency on google.golang.org/protobuf. So, to create the go.mod and go.sum file, you can run:

```
$ go mod init github.com/PacktPublishing/Protocol-Buffers-Handbook/
chapter10/makefile
$ go get google.golang.org/protobuf
$ go mod download
```

With that, you should be able to follow the rest of this chapter.

Our goal here is to have three different build systems and for all of them to be able to print the following content on stdout:

```
name: "my name"

name: "my name v1"
```

This is simple output but if we get that, this will mean we correctly generated the code for all proto files and successfully built the Go application.

Now, before actually going to more advanced build systems, let's take a step back and summarize how we use protoc and examine its limitations.

Building manually with protoc – a summary

As we saw in *Chapter 4*, we can build proto files with protoc. On top of that, protoc is also a convenient tool for learning about the Protobuf internals because we can use --encode and --decode flags. However, as with every tool out there, protoc has some limitations.

The main limitation comes when the project starts to have a lot of proto files. Let's say that you have 50 proto files you want to generate C++ code from. You will need to write a command that looks like the following:

```
$ protoc --cpp_out=. schema1.proto schema2.proto ... schema50.proto
```

You basically have to type every single file you want to generate code from and the corresponding output location with options. This means that you will have to write a huge command. And, obviously, nobody wants to do that manually.

That is why we have build tools that automatically do that for us. Let's talk about the different tools available, starting with Makefiles.

Using Makefile

> **Important message**
>
> While it is possible to use Makefiles on Windows (e.g. choco install make), this is much more a Unix thing because GNU Make is already installed on Linux and macOS. If you control the Windows environment on which the code will be running, it is totally feasible for you to use them. However, if you expect other users to run your code, this might not be the best solution.

GNU Make (https://www.gnu.org/software/make/) is a tool that lets you automate some tasks. It has a powerful syntax in which you define rules (https://www.gnu.org/software/make/manual/html_node/Rules.html) and their behavior. And later, you execute the make $target command to run the behavior you defined. Before generating code from proto files, let's see an example.

We will create a basic rule called `hello` that prints `Hello, world` on the standard output. Create a file called `Makefile` and add the following content to it:

```
hello:
    @echo "Hello, world"
```

Note that the blank before @echo is a tab, not spaces. Makefile is sensitive to these. Also, note that we add a @ before `echo` because we do not print the `echo` command itself. You can later try to remove this @ and see the difference in output.

Now, at the same directory level as the `Makefile` file, you can run the following:

```
$ make hello
```

As expected, this should output `Hello, world`.

Now that we have an idea of what this looks like, let's go deeper and start introducing Protobuf tasks. The first thing we want to do is to find all the proto files in a certain folder and its subfolders. In a Makefile, we can create a variable that contains the output of functions. These will be evaluated before the rules.

In our case, we can use the `wildcard` (https://www.gnu.org/software/make/manual/html_node/Wildcard-Function.html) function provided by make to find all the files ending with `.proto` in the `proto` folder. This would look like this (Makefile):

```
SOURCES=$(wildcard proto/*.proto proto/**/*.proto)
```

So, let's say we have the following file structure:

```
.
├─ Makefile
└─ proto
   ├─ test.proto
   └─ v1
      └─ test.proto
```

SOURCES would be a list containing both `proto/test.proto` and `proto/v1/test.proto`.

Next, in order to make a rule dependent on the generated code, we need to have the name of the generated files. Fortunately, we know that the generated file will simply have the extension `.pb.${LANG}`. For example, for go, it will be `.pb.go` and for C++ it will be `.pb.cc`.

For this, we can simply substitute the extension like so (for Go):

```
GEN=$(SOURCES:.proto=.pb.go)
```

Now that we have the sources and the names of the generated files. We can create a rule called my_ program that depends on the generated code. We do it like this:

```
my_program: $(GEN)
```

However, as you can guess, this is still not sufficient for it to work. We still need to provide the protoc command that will actually turn the proto files into generated code. For this, we will use the pattern rule (https://www.gnu.org/software/make/manual/html_node/Pattern-Rules.html), which says that a certain kind of file needs to be translated into another. In our case, we translate a proto file into a .pb.go file. Here is the rule:

```
%.pb.go : %.proto
    $(info compiling $<)
    @protoc --go_out=. --go_opt=paths=source_relative $<
```

You should recognize the protoc command, but you might not understand what is the $< sign. This is the input of the pattern rule. In this case, this is the proto file. And because this rule will be called for every file in SOURCES, we will effectively compile all the proto files.

Also, notice that we added an info message. This is totally optional, but I added it so that later, we can experiment, have a clear output, and understand what the Makefile does.

Then, as the my_program rule depends on the generated code, you can safely assume that you can use the code in .pb.go files in your application and run it in the rule. So, you could update the my_program rule like so:

```
my_program: $(GEN)
    @ go run .
```

Finally, Makefiles generally have some conventional rules called all and clean. The clean rule cleans any generated file, and the all rule is a rule that first calls clean and reruns the main rule of the makefile. In our case, this would look like the following:

```
all: clean my_program
clean:
    $(info removing $(GEN))
    @rm -f $(GEN)
```

Note that all is the default rule in a Makefile. This means that if you run the make command without any arguments, all will be run.

Having our Makefile, we should now be able to run the following:

```
$ make
```

Or we could run this:

```
$ make my_program
```

And it should output something like (without info messages):

```
name: "my name"

name: "my name v1"
```

However, the main difference between these two commands is their behavior. The make my_program command will only call the protoc command if the .pb.go file is not already generated. Try to run the command twice and you should not see the compiling step the second time. In a clean repo (without generated code), the first time, you should have the following:

```
compiling proto/test.proto
compiling proto/v1/test.proto
running app
name: "my name"

name: "my name v1"
```

And the second time, you will have the following:

```
running app
name: "my name"

name: "my name v1"
```

This is basic caching. If we do not update the schema, we do not need to recompile them.

The make command without argument, will rerun the compiling each time. This is useful if you updated the proto files and need to recompile them.

Now, let's summarize what we learned here. Makefile can automatically detect the files that we are looking for, it can build multiple languages (here, we had Go and proto), and it can have basic caching for speeding up the builds. However, Makefiles are mostly a Unix thing, and handling multiple OSes is not trivial. So, if you could not control the environment in which this would be run, you might have a hard time trying to maintain them.

Let's now see a tool that is more specific to Protobuf but provides a lot more features: Buf.

Using Buf

> **Important message**
>
> For this section, you are going to need Buf CLI. You can find how to install it here: `https://buf.build/docs/installation`.

The next tool that is important to know is Buf (`https://buf.build/`). This is mainly a CLI tool that deals with your proto files in some way. It can build them, lint them, format them, check for breaking changes, and so on. It is very interesting because it can help you with every step of the CI/CD pipeline.

Let's see an example of how to use the CLI. Let's assume that we have a similar project to what we had in the previous section:

```
.
├── go.mod
├── main.go
└── proto
    ├── test.proto
    └── v1
        └── test.proto
```

Now, at the root of the proto files (the `proto` directory), run the following command:

```
$ buf mod init
```

This should create a `buf.yaml` file in the `proto` directory. Inside this file, you will have the rules you need for checking breaking changes (`https://buf.build/docs/breaking/overview`) and linting (`https://buf.build/docs/lint/overview`).

Next, you can go to the root directory and create a file called `buf.gen.yaml` that will contain the following code:

```
version: v1
plugins:
  - name: go
    out: ./proto
    opt:
      - paths=source_relative
```

This should be very familiar because these are all the options that we passed to protoc. We use the go protoc plugin (protoc-gen-go). We generate the code in the `proto` directory, and we use the `source_relative` paths option to place the output file in the same relative directory as the input file.

With this, we can actually generate code by running the following:

```
$ buf generate proto
```

As easily as generating code, we can lint the proto files by running the following:

```
$ buf lint proto
```

If you used the proto files we used in the previous section, you should have the following output:

```
proto/test.proto:1:1:Files must have a package defined.
proto/v1/test.proto:3:1:Package name "v1" should be suffixed with a
correctly formed version, such as "v1.v1".
```

In fact, we are not following some of the linting rules here. You can comply with these rules, or you can describe the linting rules you want to follow. In `proto/buf.yaml`, you can replace this:

```
lint:
  use:
    - DEFAULT
```

You could disable some rules like this:

```
lint:
  use:
    - DEFAULT
  except:
    - PACKAGE_DEFINED
    - PACKAGE_VERSION_SUFFIX
```

You can find all the linting rules you can enable and disable in the documentation (`https://buf.build/docs/lint/rules`).

Next, you can format your proto files with the format command. Similarly, you can run:

```
$ buf format proto
```

If you do that it will print on the standard output the newly formatted files' content, but it will not rewrite your proto files. This is a safety measure. If you want to replace the content, you can add the `--write` flag. And if you want to see what is different from the original proto file, you can use the `--diff` flag. For example, you can try adding empty lines between the `syntax` statement and the option in `proto/test.proto`. Run the following:

```
$ buf format proto --diff
diff -u proto/test.proto.orig proto/test.proto
--- proto/test.proto.orig 2024-04-05 16:03:57
+++ proto/test.proto 2024-04-05 16:03:57
```

```
@@ -1,7 +1,5 @@
syntax = "proto3";


-

-

option go_package = "github.com/PacktPublishing/Protocol-Buffers-
Handbook/chapter10/buf/proto";

message Test {
```

It shows that if you allowed buf to rewrite your file, it would remove the two empty lines between the option and the syntax (the one prefixed with -). Then, as we agree to make these changes, we can run the following:

```
$ buf format proto --write
```

And now, the proto file does not contain the empty lines anymore.

Now, while I would gladly explain all the features present in Buf, there are too many for me to include them all. I recommend that you check their documentation (https://buf.build/docs/ecosystem/cli-overview). They did an excellent job at providing great features for working with proto files.

Finally, I want to touch upon how you would run the Go application we have. We need two steps:

```
$ buf generate proto
$ go run .
```

While this requires two steps, you could think about buf replacing protoc and you could also think about creating a Makefile or build script. I would argue that buf is similar to protoc but has more advanced features. It really depends on what you are looking for. If you really need linting, formatting, and so on, consider using buf; otherwise, you could keep your protoc commands.

Let's resume what we learned here. Buf is a CLI tool that can run on any OS and provide Protobuf-specific features to us. With a little bit of configuration, we can get generation, linting, formatting, and much more.

Now, let's go one step further and talk about Bazel.

Using Bazel

> **Important message**
> This section will use Bazel. In order to download it, consider using Bazelisk since it will automatically update the Bazel version to the latest LTS release. You can find how to install Bazelisk here: https://bazel.build/install/bazelisk.

The last tool that I consider worth considering is Bazel. Unlike Makefiles and Buf, Bazel is a full-blown build system. As such, it requires more configuration, but it can build multiple languages, has efficient caching, and more. Once again, let's try to run the sample project using this tool.

A modern Bazel project should start by adding a file called MODULE.bazel at the root of the directory. This file contains the dependencies that are needed to build our project. In our case, we will need to have utilities to build Protobuf and Go. We will also need to have the dependency on Protobuf Go and to manage that we will use Gazelle (https://github.com/bazelbuild/bazel-gazelle). Our MODULE.bazel looks like the following:

> **Important message**
>
> We tried to avoid as much as possible having specific versions in this book. However, the following code snippet contains versions for our dependencies. Make sure you take a look at https://registry.bazel.build/ and search for their latest version. You can search for gazelle and rules_proto and replace their versions accordingly.

```
module(
  name = "com_github_packtpublishing_protocol_buffers_handbook_
chapter10_bazel",
  version = "1.0",
)


bazel_dep(name = "gazelle", version = "0.36.0")

go_deps = use_extension("@gazelle//:extensions.bzl", "go_deps")
go_deps.from_file(go_mod = "//:go.mod")
use_repo(
  go_deps,
  "org_golang_google_protobuf"
)


bazel_dep(name = "rules_go", version = "0.46.0")
```

Note that rules in Bazel refer to a list of utilities that define how to build a certain project. rules_go here gives us the utilities for building a Go binary. Another rule, already packaged in Bazel, called rules_proto, gives us the utilities for building proto files. Also, note that we will need to have a go.mod file to tell Gazelle which dependencies to pull. In our case, the go.mod file looks like this:

```
module github.com/PacktPublishing/Protocol-Buffers-Handbook/chapter10/
bazel


go 1.22.1


require google.golang.org/protobuf v1.33.0 // indirect
```

And you can see that `google.golang.org/protobuf` is mapped to `org_golang_google_protobuf` in the `use_repo` statement (`MODULE.bazel`). In the next step, we will be able to use the latter to depend on Protobuf Go.

The next important file that we need to write is a `BUILD.bazel`. This file describes targets and how they should be built. Once described, we will be able to run/build that target from the command line by running the following:

```
$ bazel run //:target
```

At the root directory, we are going to create a `BUILD.bazel` file that contains the target called `my_program` and builds the `main.go` file. This looks like the following:

```
load("@rules_go//go:def.bzl", "go_binary")

go_binary(
  name = "my_program",
  importpath = "github.com/PacktPublishing/Protocol-Buffers-Handbook/
  chapter10/bazel",
  srcs = ["main.go"],
  deps = [
    "@org_golang_google_protobuf//encoding/prototext",
  ],
  visibility = ["//visibility:public"],
)
```

Notice that we added the dependency on prototext. This is accessible thanks to the `use_repo` statement in `MODULE.bazel`. We effectively pull out the dependency and add it to this target.

Next, we need to define targets for our proto files. This means that we need to create a `BUILD.bazel` file in proto and in proto/v1. The former looks like this:

```
load("@rules_go//go:def.bzl", "go_library")
load("@rules_go//proto:def.bzl", "go_proto_library")
load("@rules_proto//proto:defs.bzl", "proto_library")

proto_library(
  name = "test_proto",
  srcs = ["test.proto"],
)

go_proto_library(
  name = "test_go_proto",
  importpath = "github.com/PacktPublishing/Protocol-Buffers-Handbook/
  chapter10/bazel/proto",
```

```
    proto = ":test_proto",
)

go_library(
    name = "test",
    embed = [":test_go_proto"],
    importpath = "github.com/PacktPublishing/Protocol-Buffers-Handbook/
    chapter10/bazel/proto",
    visibility = ["//visibility:public"],
)
```

And the only thing that changes in the `proto/v1/BUILD.bazel` is the `importpaths`. They will be "`github.com/PacktPublishing/Protocol-Buffers-Handbook/chapter10/bazel/proto/v1`" instead of "`github.com/PacktPublishing/Protocol-Buffers-Handbook/chapter10/bazel/proto`".

From the code, you can see three targets. The first one `test_proto` represents a collection of proto files. In our case, we only have one in the current directory. The second one represents the go library made from the Go code generation on the `test_proto` target. And finally, we have a go library that can be imported by our `my_program` target.

This means we can now update `BUILD.bazel` at the root of our repo like so:

```
go_binary(
    #...
    deps = [
        "//proto:test",
        "//proto/v1:test",
        "@org_golang_google_protobuf//encoding/prototext",
    ],
)
```

The last thing we need to do before being able to run our program is to create the `go.sum` file. We can do that by running the following:

```
$ go mod download google.golang.org/protobuf
```

This is needed by Gazelle to retrieve the dependency.

Finally, we can run our `my_program` target by executing the following command:

```
$ bazel run //:my_program
```

And as expected, it should also output the following:

```
name:   "my name"

name:   "my name v1"
```

So, as you can see, Bazel built the whole application (Go and proto files) without us needing to run any other external command. Of course, it took us more configuration, but in the long term, it might be worth considering having such a build system.

On last thing that I want to mention is that this section is in no way an extensive tutorial on Bazel. This build system is highly configurable, and our sample project is pretty small. Before going all-in in using Bazel, be sure to check whether this is worth it. Bazel generally shines for bigger projects and for monorepos.

Now, let's summarize what we learned in this section. Bazel is a full-blown build system that can, after configuration, build a project containing multiple languages. The most attractive part of this tool is that we can run a simple `bazel run //:target` command and all the dependencies and source code will be built.

Summary

In this chapter, we saw three popular ways of building Protobuf projects. The first one was using some kind of automation tool, such as Makefile. The second used the highly specialized tool called Buf. And the third one was using the highly generalized build system called Bazel. All of these have some advantages and disadvantages, and our job as engineers is to decide which tool is right for the job.

This book ends with this chapter. I hope you have learned something from all the theory and the practical parts. Protobuf is a very interesting data format, and with the rise of gRPC, Protobuf has become a must-have skill. With this book, you have learned everything from the serialization internals to how to use Protobuf in Python and Golang. I hope you liked the adventure, and I hope it will help you during your career.

Challenge

- Try adding one of the build systems to the AddressBook in Golang.
- Do the same with the AddressBook in Python.
- Try to create a project in your favorite programming language and build it with one, two, or all of the build systems shown in this chapter.

Index

Symbols

A

B

C

packtpub.com

Subscribe to our online digital library for full access to over 7,000 books and videos, as well as industry leading tools to help you plan your personal development and advance your career. For more information, please visit our website.

Why subscribe?

- Spend less time learning and more time coding with practical eBooks and Videos from over 4,000 industry professionals

- Improve your learning with Skill Plans built especially for you

- Get a free eBook or video every month

- Fully searchable for easy access to vital information

- Copy and paste, print, and bookmark content

Did you know that Packt offers eBook versions of every book published, with PDF and ePub files available? You can upgrade to the eBook version at packtpub.com and as a print book customer, you are entitled to a discount on the eBook copy. Get in touch with us at customercare@packtpub.com for more details.

At www.packtpub.com, you can also read a collection of free technical articles, sign up for a range of free newsletters, and receive exclusive discounts and offers on Packt books and eBooks.

Other Books You May Enjoy

If you enjoyed this book, you may be interested in these other books by Packt:

Go Programming - From Beginner to Professional

Samantha Coyle

ISBN: 978-1-80324-305-4

- Understand the Go syntax and apply it proficiently to handle data and write functions
- Debug your Go code to troubleshoot development problems
- Safely handle errors and recover from panics
- Implement polymorphism using interfaces and gain insight into generics
- Work with files and connect to popular external databases
- Create an HTTP client and server and work with a RESTful web API
- Use concurrency to design efficient software
- Use Go tools to simplify development and improve your code

gRPC Go for Professionals

Clément Jean

ISBN: 978-1-83763-884-0

- Understand the different API endpoints that gRPC lets you write
- Discover the essential considerations when writing your Protobuf files
- Compile Protobuf code with protoc and Bazel for efficient development
- Gain insights into how advanced gRPC concepts work
- Grasp techniques for unit testing and load testing your API
- Get to grips with deploying your microservices with Docker and Kubernetes
- Discover tools for writing secure and efficient gRPC code

Packt is searching for authors like you

If you're interested in becoming an author for Packt, please visit `authors.packtpub.com` and apply today. We have worked with thousands of developers and tech professionals, just like you, to help them share their insight with the global tech community. You can make a general application, apply for a specific hot topic that we are recruiting an author for, or submit your own idea.

Share Your Thoughts

Now you've finished *Protocol Buffers Handbook*, we'd love to hear your thoughts! Scan the QR code below to go straight to the Amazon review page for this book and share your feedback or leave a review on the site that you purchased it from.

`https://packt.link/r/1805124676`

Your review is important to us and the tech community and will help us make sure we're delivering excellent quality content.

Download a free PDF copy of this book

Thanks for purchasing this book!

Do you like to read on the go but are unable to carry your print books everywhere?

Is your eBook purchase not compatible with the device of your choice?

Don't worry, now with every Packt book you get a DRM-free PDF version of that book at no cost.

Read anywhere, any place, on any device. Search, copy, and paste code from your favorite technical books directly into your application.

The perks don't stop there, you can get exclusive access to discounts, newsletters, and great free content in your inbox daily

Follow these simple steps to get the benefits:

1. Scan the QR code or visit the link below

https://packt.link/free-ebook/978-1-80512-467-2

2. Submit your proof of purchase

3. That's it! We'll send your free PDF and other benefits to your email directly

www.ingramcontent.com/pod-product-compliance
Lightning Source LLC
LaVergne TN
LVHW081523050326
832903LV00025B/1610